PICASSO

Masterworks from The Museum of Modern Art

PICASSO

*Masterworks from
The Museum of Modern Art*

An exhibition organized by
The Museum of Modern Art
in collaboration with the
Los Angeles County Museum of Art

KIRK VARNEDOE

PEPE KARMEL

The Museum of Modern Art, New York

Published on the occasion of the exhibition *Picasso: Masterworks from The Museum of Modern Art,* shown at the Los Angeles County Museum of Art, September 6, 1998–January 4, 1999. The exhibition was directed by Kirk Varnedoe, Chief Curator, and Pepe Karmel, Adjunct Assistant Curator, Department of Painting and Sculpture, The Museum of Modern Art, New York.

Picasso: Masterworks from The Museum of Modern Art was organized by The Museum of Modern Art, New York, in collaboration with the Los Angeles County Museum of Art, the High Museum of Art, Atlanta, and the National Gallery of Canada, Ottawa.

All works of Pablo Picasso © 1997 Estate of Pablo Picasso/Artists Rights Society (ARS), N.Y.

Produced by the Department of Publications
The Museum of Modern Art, New York
Edited by Barbara Ross
Designed by Antony Drobinski, Emsworth Design, New York
Production by Marc Sapir
Printed and bound by Amilcare Pizzi S.p.A., Milan

Published by The Museum of Modern Art
11 West 53 Street, New York, New York 10019

Printed in Italy

COVER: Pablo Picasso. *Girl Before a Mirror*. Boisgeloup, March 1932. Oil on canvas, 64 × 51¼" (162.3 x 130.2 cm). The Museum of Modern Art, New York. Gift of Mrs. Simon Guggenheim

FRONTISPIECE: Picasso in his studio at 242, boulevard Raspail, Paris, early 1913. Musée Picasso, Paris, Picasso Archives

CONTENTS

FOREWORD

The Museum of Modern Art is often referred to as "the house that Pablo built." By 1929, when the Museum opened, Picasso had already established himself as the most influential figure in modern art. Our first exhibition of twentieth-century European art, in 1930, included fifteen of his works. In the same year, our founding director, Alfred H. Barr, Jr., began planning a retrospective devoted exclusively to Picasso. Logistical difficulties prevented the immediate realization of this project, but Picasso played a major role in Barr's groundbreaking surveys of 1936, *Cubism and Abstract Art* and *Fantastic Art, Dada, Surrealism*: he was represented by twenty-nine paintings, drawings, and sculptures in the first, and by an additional thirteen works in the second.

Barr's Picasso retrospective finally opened in November 1939. Including over 360 paintings, sculptures, drawings, and prints, it demonstrated the extraordinary range and diversity of Picasso's work, confirming both his preeminence as an artist and the Museum's preeminence as a standard-bearer for modern art. Recognizing the Museum's commitment to his work, the artist left his antiwar masterpiece of 1937, *Guernica*, on extended loan here, specifying that it should be given to Spain when and if democracy returned to the land of his birth. (It was sent to Madrid, with mingled joy and regret, in 1981, and is now housed in the Reina Sofía Art Center there.)

After World War II, The Museum of Modern Art continued to explore Picasso's achievements. His seventy-fifth birthday, in 1957, was celebrated with another retrospective, his eightieth and ninetieth birthdays with exhibitions drawn from the Museum's ever-growing collection of his work. Other exhibitions documented his remarkable activity as a printmaker, while *The Sculpture of Picasso*, in 1967, revealed an aspect of his work that had remained virtually unknown despite his fame as a painter. In 1980, seven years after the artist's death, the Museum devoted its entire gallery space to *Pablo Picasso: A Retrospective*. Organized by William Rubin, Barr's successor as Director of Painting and Sculpture, this mammoth exhibition (including more than nine hundred paintings, sculptures, drawings, collages, prints, ceramics, and theater designs) attracted over one million visitors. Nine years later, in *Picasso and Braque: Pioneering Cubism*, Rubin explored the most abstract phase of the artist's career. Conversely, his 1996 exhibition, *Picasso and Portraiture: Representation and Transformation*, demonstrated the range of human emotion in the artist's work.

As the first overview of Picasso's career since the retrospective of 1980, this exhibition offers a valuable opportunity to reconsider the significance of the artist's oeuvre. It also allows us to bring together key works that are usually separated in our permanent collection galleries. Here, exceptionally, the visitor can move in rapid succession from one masterwork to another: from the classical naturalism of *Boy Leading a Horse* (1906) to the Cubist facets of *Girl with a Mandolin* (1910), the sensual abstraction of *Girl Before a Mirror* (1932), and the terrifying anatomy of *Woman Dressing Her Hair* (1940). We are particularly happy to have an opportunity to integrate these well-known paintings with superb examples of Picasso's drawings, prints, and sculptures.

It is also gratifying that the exhibition documents more than sixty-five years of generous donations, from the gouache *Head* (1909) given by Mrs. Saidie A. May in 1930 to the oil painting of *Woman Dressing Her Hair* received in 1995 as part of the Louise Reinhardt Smith bequest. The cardboard maquette for *Guitar* (1912)—the first constructed sculpture in the history of modern art—was given to the Museum by the artist himself in 1972; the portrait of *Maya in a Sailor Suit* (1938) was donated by his widow in 1985, "in honor," as she said, "of the Museum's continuous commitment to Pablo Picasso's art."

A program of circulating exhibitions and loans to other museums has long accompanied the program of exhibitions at The Museum of Modern Art. We are pleased to be able to present *Picasso: Masterworks from The Museum of Modern Art* at the Los Angeles County Museum of Art, after its appearances at the High Museum of Art, Atlanta, and the National Gallery of Canada, Ottawa. *Picasso: Masterworks* follows in the footsteps of numerous earlier exhibitions that have traveled from our Museum to the Los Angeles County Museum of Art. In just the last five years, these have included *Roy DeCarava: A Retrospective, Kandinsky: Compositions, John Heartfield: Photomontages, The William S. Paley Collection*, and *Pleasures and Terrors of Domestic Comfort*. In the same time period, MoMA and LACMA have also collaborated on the organization of two important exhibitions of contemporary art, *Annette Messager* and *Love Forever: Yayoi Kusama, 1958–1968*.

It has been a pleasure to work once again with Graham W. J. Beal, Director of the Los Angeles County Museum of Art, and with Lynn Zelevansky, Associate Curator of Modern and Contemporary Art at Los Angeles (and formerly a valued member of the Modern's staff). We are also grateful to all those in Atlanta and Ottawa who originally made this exhibition possible. At the High Museum of Art, Atlanta, we would particularly like to thank Ned Rifkin, Nancy and Holcombe T. Green, Jr., Director; Michael E. Shapiro, Deputy Director and Chief Curator; and Carrie Przybilla, Curator of Modern and Contemporary Art. At the National Gallery of Art, Ottawa, we want to acknowledge former and present directors Shirley L. Thomson and Pierre Théberge; Yves Dagenais, Deputy Director; Colin Bailey, Chief Curator; and Brydon Smith, Curator of Modern Art.

At The Museum of Modern Art, the organization of this exhibition has called on the efforts of numerous members of our dedicated staff. Kirk Varnedoe, Chief Curator in the Department of Painting and Sculpture, originally proposed a series of exhibitions drawn from our collections; between Matisse and Picasso, the series has gotten off to a splendid start. In collaboration with Pepe Karmel, Adjunct Assistant Curator, Department of Painting and Sculpture, he directed, and wrote the catalogue for, the current exhibition. The selection of drawings and prints was made with the assistance of Margit Rowell, Chief Curator, Department of Drawings, and Deborah Wye, Chief Curator, Department of Prints and Illustrated Books. The curators of the exhibition received crucial support from Jennifer Russell, Deputy Director for Exhibitions and Collections Support; Elizabeth Addison, Deputy Director for Marketing and Communications; Linda Thomas, Coordinator of Exhibitions; Ramona Bronkar Bannayan, former Associate Registrar; Jana Joyce, Assistant Registrar; and Harriet Schoenholz Bee, Managing Editor, Department of Publications.

Glenn D. Lowry
Director, The Museum of Modern Art

PREFACE

Although many art museums around the world have strong holdings in the work of particular artists or art movements, it is probably fair to say that none surpasses New York's Museum of Modern Art in the breadth and depth of its collection of work by Picasso. As Glenn Lowry points out in his foreword, the growth of MoMA closely paralleled the general recognition of Picasso as this century's most influential artist (an intellectually unfashionable notion today perhaps, but one that challenged and intimidated other artists until very recently). The Museum of Modern Art's collection grew with the active participation of the artist right up until his death. Indeed, I remember William Rubin in 1980 relaying the delightful anecdote that when, to celebrate his own ninetieth birthday, Picasso gave the Museum the metal version of his revolutionary Cubist sculpture *Guitar*, the artist committed himself to give another such work on each of his birthdays for the next ten years!

As it happens, for conservation reasons the metal *Guitar* is not included in this presentation; it is represented here by Picasso's groundbreaking cardboard maquette. For the same reasons, Picasso's great 1907 painting *Les Demoiselles d'Avignon,* is also absent; a trip to New York is necessary to see this convention-shattering work. Despite these absences, the 117 paintings, drawings, sculptures, and prints in *Picasso: Masterworks from The Museum of Modern Art* comprise virtually a complete retrospective, offering quintessential works from each of the protean artist's periods and reflecting his general shift in emphasis over the decades from painting to sculpture, drawing, and printmaking.

This exhibition represents a rare opportunity for the Los Angeles County Museum of Art to present to its public such a complete representation of Picasso's work, and I am grateful to Glenn D. Lowry, Director of The Museum of Modern Art, for offering the exhibition to us. I would also like to thank Ned Rifkin, Director of the High Museum of Art, Atlanta; and Shirley L. Thomson, former Director, and Pierre Théberge, Director of the National Gallery of Canada, Ottawa, for their gracious consent in adding LACMA to the itinerary of an exhibition originally planned exclusively for their institutions. The exhibition was organized by Kirk Varnedoe, Chief Curator, and Pepe Karmel, Adjunct Assistant Curator, Department of Painting and Sculpture, The Museum of Modern Art. In fact, LACMA's presentation differs from those of the previous venues, reflecting, in part, the commitment of two works to another exhibition and their replacement by several other superb pictures, but also the participation of Lynn Zelevansky, Associate Curator of Modern and Contemporary Art at LACMA. Prior to her appointment here, Lynn was Curatorial Assistant at The Museum of Modern Art, where, among other duties, she worked with William Rubin on the 1989 exhibition *Picasso and Braque: Pioneering Cubism.* We are fortunate to have on our curatorial staff a person with such knowledge of the material, and I am grateful to Lynn for adding this project to an already heavy curatorial load. She, in turn, joins me in expressing thanks to Kirk Varnedoe and Pepe Karmel as well as to Jennifer Russell, MoMA's Deputy Director for Exhibitions and Collections Support, for their work in reshaping the exhibition for its Los Angeles showing. Finally, I would like to acknowledge the contributions—some large, some small but all, in their way, crucial—from all the individuals associated with this exhibition, whose names appear in the Acknowledgments on page 149.

Graham W. J. Beal
Director, Los Angeles County Museum of Art

Picasso in Paris, 1904
Photograph by Ricardo Canals, inscribed:
"A mes chers amis Suzanne et Henri [Bloch],
Picasso, 1904"

RETHINKING PICASSO TODAY

Kirk Varnedoe

The literature on Picasso is vast: his life has been exhaustively chronicled by historians, lovers, and friends, and his work is extensively published, from the smallest juvenile scraps to the grandest canvases. No other artist, from any period, has received such attention in his or her lifetime, and few have ever been the focus of similar lionization. Yet there have been, and continue to be, broad disagreements about *why* Picasso should be considered so special, and studied so intently. Early in his career, the matter seemed simple: he was a quick study, and something of a prodigy. As a beginning student, he learned with precocious swiftness to perform conventional exercises, such as drawing a plaster torso with the proper shadows (fig. 1). And when as a teenager he began to paint large canvases, his choice of sentimental themes and his command of the formulae of successful academic painters showed that he had a ready facility for adopting and exploiting the approved styles of the day. Even in his first forays into more radical styles of painting, it was his rapid adaptation of the signature styles of French avant-garde painters that made him seem both a dexterous thief and a remarkable talent. His friend Max Jacob later remembered that, after his first show in

1. *Pablo Picasso*
STUDY OF A TORSO, AFTER A PLASTER CAST.
La Coruña, 1894–95
Charcoal, 19⅜ × 12⅜" (49 × 31.5 cm)
Zervos VI, 1. Musée Picasso, Paris

2. *Pablo Picasso*

LES DEMOISELLES D'AVIGNON. Paris, begun May,
reworked July 1907

Oil on canvas, 96 × 92" (243.9 × 233.7 cm)
Zervos II*, 18. D.R. 47. The Museum of Modern Art,
New York. Acquired through the Lillie P. Bliss Bequest

Paris, Picasso "was accused of imitating Steinlen, Vuillard, Van Gogh, etc., but everyone recognized that he had a fire, a real brilliance, a painter's eye."[1]

The pathos-soaked works of the Blue Period then showed a more personal combination of academic drawing and avant-garde license with a mournfully monochrome palette; but their Symbolist cast looked *retardataire* in the Parisian avant-garde of the early 1900s, and made Picasso, barely in his twenties, seem old before his time. It was with less sentimental and lightened Rose Period works like *Boy Leading a Horse* (plate, p. 43) that he began establishing his credentials with progressive collectors, partly on the basis of an evidently simplifying, even archaizing, delineation of the human form. With his next step into a more extreme "primitivism," however, and especially with the brutally explosive canvas of the *Demoiselles d'Avignon* (fig. 2), Picasso began not only to challenge the boldest of his fellow painters, but to change the basic terms on which his talent could be understood. The "fire" that Jacob described erupted more plainly than ever, but without any grounding in the familiar styles or conventions of accepted art; Picasso's contemporaries were confronted no longer with recognizable skill or facility, but with profoundly unsettling originality. From that moment onward, through more than sixty years of near-constant twists and turns, and to the present day, astonished observers of this unparalleled career have scrambled to find appropriate ways to elucidate the phenomenon of Picasso's singular creativity.

When an artist shatters so many rules and expectations, what criteria can de devised by which to judge him, or to praise his accomplishment? As Picasso began to take greater liberties with color, proportion, space, and anatomy, his advocates had to move into more problematic terrains of persuasion to commend his merits. Beginning especially with the drastic innovations of Cubism (for example, *The Architect's Table* of 1912; plate, p. 61), those who were subjectively drawn to Picasso's art often sought to justify it in objective terms, recasting apparently whimsical inventions as absolutes, and repudiations of observed reality as representations of a higher reality. Not only critics but fellow artists found in Cubism what they thought were connections to the evidence of x-rays, the mystic harmonics of occult geometries, or the new theories of n-dimensional space or Einsteinian relativity.[2] And aesthetic theorists often insisted that a parallel kind of necessity or inevitability, internal to the history of art, governed the emergence of these new languages of form. In this, Picasso's case was hardly unique: "scientific," "spiritual," or "timeless, objective" qualities were commonly evoked in the polemics that sought to promote modern art before World War II, when it remained the embattled pursuit of a relatively restricted avant-garde. In more recent years, though, when modern art has been routinely accepted as an established (if not an "establishment") enterprise, with Picasso as one of its grand masters, the interest of his work has been explained quite differently.

Especially in the quarter-century since Picasso's death, there has been a sea change in the way his art is approached. Formerly, he was touted for abandoning slavish mimesis and literary narratives and leading the way toward a new art of purer form, divorced from the need to resemble things or relate tales. His art, like modern art in general, was said to represent a

3. *Pablo Picasso*
TABLE WITH BOTTLE, WINEGLASS, AND NEWSPAPER.
Paris, after December 4, 1912
Pasted paper, charcoal, and gouache, 24⅜ × 18⅞" (62 × 48 cm)
D.R. 542. Musée National d'Art Moderne, Centre National d'Art
et de Culture Georges Pompidou, Paris. Gift of Henri Laugier

triumph of style over story, code over content. As such, it was implicitly held to epitomize the larger struggle to escape tradition's stifling bonds and dwell in an unsentimental, unfamiliar, and denuded realm of ideals appropriate to modern life's promises of human and social renovation. Lately, however, we tend to see Picasso's connections to his epoch less idealistically, and to describe them less in the abstract than in the concrete. Where, for example, earlier historians looked at the fragmented letters in Cubist collages as formal devices that emphasized the spacelessly flat nature of the surfaces, Robert Rosenblum showed in a 1973 article that these scraps of newspapers could be *read*, both as evidence of Picasso's punning games with language and as texts on the topical issues that swirled around the artist at the time of World War I.[3] (Thus, the headline "Un Coup de Théâtre" [a theatrical event or gesture] could be truncated to suggest "Un Coup[e] de Thé" [a cup of tea] in a café-table still life [fig. 3]; and this, as well as more evidently bellicose headlines and texts Picasso clipped, were also references to savage battles in the Balkans.) Since then, a similar shift in approach has marked a flood tide of more literal "readings" that attempt to decipher Picasso's works, in all periods, as coded markers for his position within the changing cultural and political frameworks of his time.[4]

Meanwhile, virtually nothing has been said recently about the "objective" or "universal" properties of Picasso's art; instead, we find writers striving to draw ever more direct, causal links between his pictures and the particulars of his life—especially his love life. It is easy now to forget that, prior to the 1970s, the specific erotic content of Picasso's work was of relatively minor importance in the literature on the artist, and the names and dates of his romantic attachments were barely dealt with. Now, we routinely interpret the distorted "monsters" in paintings of the late 1920s as images of his wife Olga Khokhlova, turned into a shrieking harridan by her alienation and anger over the breakdown of their marriage; and it has become almost a cliché for scholars, when writing on Picasso, to contrast these bony horrors, like illustrations in a romantic drama, with the swelling, sensuous forms of the paintings of the early 1930s, taken as direct expressions of the artist's blissful erotic fulfillment with his new young mistress, Marie-Thérèse Walter (see *Face of Marie-Thérèse* and *Girl Before a Mirror;* plates, pp. 99, 101).[5] Almost inevitably, questions have also been raised as to the value we should place on such art, if we see it as born directly from a life history so often marked by apparently imperious domination of, or cruelty toward, women.

Perhaps most basically, we now examine Picasso's work with the idea, not that style overcomes story, but that style *is* story. In other words, we tend to seek definable motivations, even sublimated narratives, in what were formerly seen as the "purely formal" aspects of Picasso's inventions. Ever since Leo Steinberg showed in masterful fashion that the radical formal innovations of the *Demoiselles d'Avignon* did not simply supplant its initial, moralizing theme of sex and death, but instead acted to engage the viewer with these same anxieties in more complex, intense, and challenging ways,[6] the fundamental split between "autonomous" form and storytelling content has been blurred; and writers now search much more frequently to explain even the artist's most abstract passages as oblique encodings of, rather than flights from, particular messages of meaning.

This new ferment of research and interpretation has expanded Picasso's reputation and his literature tremendously, and won new audiences for him. But it can often seem a hollow gain, in which the allegedly encoded content, not the art at hand, becomes the primary point of interest; and in which the man's celebrity itself seems enough to license, in self-perpetuation, adulatory attention to his life (or in which the life is used, in reverse, as the moral measure of the art). In treating Picasso as an academic industry or a popular shibboleth, recent commentators may tend to take for granted or ignore more testy questions as to why and in what ways, independently of the anecdotes of its origins or originator, the art deserves our admiration and long-term attention. Such basic judgments of value seem now to be addressed less often by supporters than by critics, who fume that the art does *not* deserve it—that the whole booming enterprise of Picasso-adulation is a corrupt sham perpetrated on a gullible public.

We may think this kind of tirade belongs only to an unenlightened or intolerant past; the triumph over such fustian early resistance, is after all, an essential part of the romance of any modern artist's ascent. But the anti-Picasso position is more than just an amusing relic of bygone days: it has been a constant factor straight through the chronicle of his career and its aftermath, and is still very much alive today. This opposition—with modernist and antimodernist wings, and resonances on the political left and right—has its own rich history of developing variations. And within this history, intriguingly, some of Picasso's most impressive enemies have in fact been erstwhile friends, turned apostates. Already early on, when no less an intimate than Georges Braque characterized Picasso's bravado powers of astonishment by saying he was like one who imbibed kerosene in order to spit fire, hostile skepticism was patent in the implied analogy with flame-belching street performers—all quick flash, empty dazzle, and entertainment.[7] An ardent early patron, Leo Stein, expressed the kind of disillusionment that has often echoed since: in his view, Picasso was an artist almost over-gifted with talent and imagination, who had a golden early moment but then squandered his potential through undisciplined self-indulgence, and loss of contact with the broader audience that might have been his. For Stein, a fan of the Rose Period, that fall came very early indeed, with the onset of Cubism.[8] But others, holding Cubism to be Picasso's finest hour, look to its end as the sunset, lamenting the regression into neoclassicism and subsequent lack of challenge and restraint.[9] And still others have found the work of the 1920s and 1930s fully vigorous and fertile, but have averred that *Guernica* (fig. 4), the huge 1937 mural denouncing the aerial bombing of a Basque town by the fascists during the Spanish Civil War, marks the crucial turning point. *Guernica* has been seen by some critics as a last great burst of noble, socially conscious ambition, and by others as a plunge into solipsism and weary props; but in both cases it is frequently chosen to mark the starting point of a downward slide in the artist's powers.[10] Whatever the chronological focus, throughout this literature weaves the

4. *Pablo Picasso*
GUERNICA. Paris, May–early June, 1937
Oil on canvas, 11′6″ × 25′8″ (350.5 × 782.3 cm)
Zervos IX, 65. Reina Sofia Art Center, Madrid

complex fervor of love betrayed, and the consistent stereotype of an artist who started well and went wrong because of flaws deeply interwoven with his talents—a creator ultimately too lavishly gifted, too independent, too freely inventive, for his own (or our) good.

Such sniping may leave us with a very cranky body of opinion, but it is not simple-minded, and it often makes better—and more revealing—reading than many emptily undiscriminating advocacies. Recently, for example, an astute study of contemporary reactions to Picasso's Cubism has shown that it was not the fans and promoters (who argued for connections to Plato and n-dimensional physics) but the unconvinced mockers and nay-sayers (who thought they saw connections to cheap cabaret humor) who ultimately had a more telling, insightful grasp on the principles of the art at hand.[11] In this case, as in others, if we ignore those aspects of Picasso on which the doubters harp, we surely truncate our subject. Not just in some simplistic equation of personality and painting, but closer to the center of the artistic achievement itself, Picasso's formidable capacity for revelation and his facile showmanship closely cohabited, just as his fearless, instinctual self-reliance had as its flip side a frequently uncritical self-indulgence, his force of passion twinned with his weakness for sentiment and his profound seriousness as an artist was often inseparable from his raunchy schoolboy humor. Fascination with difficult magic and doubts about easy play will likely never be—and never should be—extricated one from the other in our attempts to come to terms with the man and his legacy. It is worth considering, though, that the frequency of friend-turned-enemy among Picasso's critics suggests that he himself may have made the rules, or raised the level of expectations, by which he has sometimes been deemed to fail. Moreover, in the course of modern art, one of Picasso's most important roles may have been a negatively charged one, of provoking contestation or opposition: some very potent sparks of both modern creativity and modern criticism have, for a long time now, been caused by striking against the flint of the models of art and artmaking that Picasso provided.

Criticism, of course, often involves comparative judgment, and those who deny Picasso's preeminence in their accounts of twentieth-century art often do so competitively, in order to champion another creator or an alternative strain. Perhaps the two most dominant nemeses proposed have been Henri Matisse, in the first half of the century, and Marcel Duchamp since. The rivalry between the painter of the *Dance* and the painter of the *Demoiselles* was traditionally seen as a yin-yang relation between (as Matisse himself once said) the North and South poles of the art of their time—Picasso the sterner master of line, structure, and the dark forces of the psyche, versus Matisse the lyric poet of untrammeled color and joy, with all the attendant polarizations between "masculine" ratiocination and "feminine," sensual decoration.[12] Yet in another context, Picasso assured an interviewer that an astute analysis of their crucial early innovations would show that, from 1905 to 1907, he and Matisse were in fact doing the same things by different means;[13] and their subsequent careers show countless instances in which these artists, whose temperaments were seemingly so opposed, fed off each other, responded one to the other, and knowingly criss-crossed shared terrain in dialogue. Without Matisse's absorption of Cubism (compare Picasso's *Man with a Hat* of 1912 [plate, p. 67] with Matisse's *White and Pink Head* of 1914–15 [fig. 5]), or Picasso's response to Matisse's senses of color and of exoticism—to cite only some obvious points of exchange—neither artist would have produced many of the achievements we know as their signature works. Even after Matisse's death in 1954, the exchange continued: commenting on his rephrasings of Eugène Delacroix's 1834 harem scene,

5. *Henri Matisse*
WHITE AND PINK HEAD. Paris, fall 1914–15
Oil on canvas, 29½ × 18½ (75 × 47 cm)
Musée National d'Art Moderne, Centre National d'Art et de Culture Georges Pompidou, Paris

6. *Henri Matisse*
LARGE RECLINING NUDE/THE PINK NUDE.
Nice, late April–October 31, 1935
Oil on canvas, 26 × 36½" (66 × 92.7 cm)
The Baltimore Museum of Art. The Cone Collec-
tion, formed by Dr. Claribel Cone and Miss Etta
Cone of Baltimore, Maryland

Les Femmes d'Alger (The Women of Algiers), Picasso said, "Matisse left me his odalisques" (figs. 6, 7).[14]

A more profound rift divides Picasso from Duchamp, the instigator of "readymade" art such as the urinal titled *Fountain* (which he submitted to a 1917 exhibition) and the artist whose rising prestige has seemed to provide Picasso's legacy with its most formidable challenge—in terms of influence on and relevance to contemporary work—in the last four decades. Dissatisfied with formalist theories of modern art in which Picasso was often lionized, and leery of the robust confidence, heavy sensual engagement, and volcanic, hands-on productivity Picasso's oeuvre seems to embody, a great many contemporary artists have found a more intellectually respectable basis for their work in Duchamp's hands-off parsimony of gesture, his esoteric and ambiguous sexual imagery, and his sardonically subversive questioning of art's contexts and rules. In many schematized theoretical accounts, Picasso the protean fabricator and form-giver is now often presented as a paragon of "classic modernism," in opposition to the "postmodernism" that claims as a prime source Duchamp's more coolly ironic, conceptually based, antiaesthetic strategies. Yet, as with the earlier case of Matisse, we should not easily accede to such simplistic polarizations, which not only cheat the several elements of cerebral, "Duchampian" strategy at play in parts of Picasso's work, but also tend—falsely—to make Picasso emblematic of a "modernism" to which he may just as rightly be seen as a glaring exception.

Without arguing fatuously that Picasso was unique, without context, and sui generis, it is useful—just as it is instructive to listen to his detractors as well as his supporters—to reflect on all the ways in which he was *not* a representative modern artist. He never, for example, embraced abstraction, which, from Kasimir Malevich and Piet Mondrian to Jackson Pollock and Richard Serra, has represented one of the central, recurrent vehicles of modern expression, and indeed, one of the defining pursuits of modernism in the arts. He also spurned the modern spirit in architecture and design, preferring throughout his life to live in older buildings, accumulating traditional furniture and often using antique frames for his work. And given the context of a life that began in an era of horse carriages and ended after men walked on the moon, there is remarkably little evidence in his art—beyond

7. *Pablo Picasso*
WOMEN OF ALGIERS, AFTER DELACROIX.
Paris, February 11, 1955
Oil on canvas, 51¼ × 76¾" (130 × 195 cm)
Zervos XVI, 357. Victor W. Ganz Trust

the newspaper clippings and advertising detritus of Cubist collages in the 1910s—of contact with anything specifically connected to twentieth-century mechanical or industrial innovations. Loyal to many folkloric superstitions learned in childhood, Picasso had an equally firm antipathy to the rationalist, scientific spirit that for so many of his contemporaries formed such an important part of modernity's promise. His often-quoted maxim, "I do not search, I find," can be understood in this context as reflecting his disdain for the notion of a work of art as an act of research or an experiment.[15] In these and other respects—his lifelong devotion to Mediterranean classicism as a recurrent touchstone, his refusal to conform to any linear notion of progress in his artistic development—Picasso's position as a prime mover in modern art, along with his insistent singularities, belie any pat definition of a unified, coherent modern*ism*. It may in fact be his "conservative" compromises and exceptionalism—in his concessions to a residual naturalism, in his retention of the simplified codes of caricature, in his bawdy humor and urge to storytelling, even in the strain of vulgarity that haunts his aesthetic—that has helped gain for his art a broader audience and a more popular appeal than other modern artists have enjoyed, and that has, ironically, secured his position as the king of the hill, the paradigmatic figure in the field.

8. *Pablo Picasso*
PROJECT FOR A MONUMENT. Dinard, July 30, 1928
India ink on paper, 11 ¹³⁄₁₆ × 8 ¹¹⁄₁₆" (30 × 22 cm)
Zervos VII, 204. Marina Picasso Collection, Courtesy Jan Krugier Gallery, New York

9. *Henry Moore*
FOUR-PIECE COMPOSITION (RECLINING FIGURES). 1934
Cumberland alabaster, 6 ⅞ × 18 × 8"
(17.5 × 45.7 × 20.3 cm)
The Trustees of the Tate Gallery

If Picasso is, however, an inappropriate flag bearer for the whole of the modern movement in the visual arts, he is at the same time an indispensable and pervasive presence in that history. No other single figure has had so widespread and profound an influence on both painting and sculpture in this century, nor exercised a talent so impressively across such a wide course of time and range of mediums. Passing moments in his development were enough to focus lifelong pursuits in the work of others: the briefest contact with Picasso's art could spawn whole careers, or shape decisive changes in an artist's stature. One visit to the Paris studio, for example, was sufficient to send Vladimir Tatlin back to prerevolutionary Russia with the impetus that shaped his most radical constructions; and even by long distance, through the publication of sketches for his new "anatomies" in the 1920s and 1930s, Picasso could decisively mark the careers of artists as far-flung as Henry Moore (figs. 8, 9), David Smith (figs. 10, 11), and Pollock. Yet, where Moore saw a vocabulary of monumental, telluric repose, Pollock and others found the stuff of violent struggle and hieratic confrontation. Similarly, while the Futurists had found Picasso's Cubism the goad to celebrations of movement and explosively destructive force, Mondrian looked at the same pictures and saw the scaffolding for an art of purified balance and

10. *Pablo Picasso*
WOMAN IN THE GARDEN. Paris, early 1929
Welded iron, painted white, 81⅛ × 46 × 33½"
(206 × 117 × 85 cm)
Spies 72(I). Musée Picasso, Paris

11. *David Smith*
LEDA. 1938
Steel, painted brown, 28⅝ × 13½ × 15½"
(72.7 × 34.3 × 39.4 cm)
Museum of Fine Arts, Houston. Gift of Mr. and Mrs. W. D. Hawkins

12. *Giacomo Balla*
SPEEDING AUTOMOBILE. 1912
Oil on wood, 21⅞ × 27⅛" (55.6 × 68.9 cm)
The Museum of Modern Art, New York. Purchase

13. *Piet Mondrian*
PIER AND OCEAN. 1914
*Charcoal and white watercolor on buff paper,
34⅝ × 44" (87.9 × 111.2 cm)
The Museum of Modern Art, New York. Mrs.
Simon Guggenheim Fund*

harmony (compare *The Architect's Table* with figs. 12 and 13). In such ways, not from one but from many, conflicting motives, which speak for the depth and complexity of his work, Picasso was the pacesetter, the "man to beat"— mentor and target, idol or demon—for a great many of the most important artists who developed the lineages of modern art between 1910 and the early 1950s; Willem de Kooning's *Woman* series of that latter period (fig. 14) still finds itself grappling directly with the provocation of the *Demoiselles d'Avignon*. If after 1955 Picasso became less an immediate competitor and more a distant source, he has continued to resonate, notably, for example, in the work of Jasper Johns—whose work of the 1980s and early 1990s openly and frequently "quotes" from Picasso's motifs of the 1930s and later (figs. 15,

16)—and in the work of numerous other contemporary creators.[16] And just as Picasso formed often-unlikely hybrids of forebears such as Paul Cézanne and Henri Rousseau (see *Fruit Dish*; plate, p. 49), these artists have fused Picasso's lessons with those of Duchamp and other seeming antagonists to develop unexpected new aspects of his still-vital descendancy.

In the worlds of scholarship and criticism, Picasso drew to himself in his lifetime the very best minds at work in the early formation of modern art history, and then their immediate students and followers—Alfred H. Barr, Jr., Clement Greenberg, and Meyer Schapiro for example, in one generation, then Robert Rosenblum, William Rubin, and Leo Steinberg, among others, in the next. Since his death, younger generations of writers and researchers have only begun to absorb the volumes of new information, and the panoply of fresh possibilities, revealed in the myriad sketchbooks,

14. *Willem de Kooning*
WOMAN, I. 1950–52
Oil on canvas, 6' 3 7/8" × 58" (192.7 × 147.3 cm)
The Museum of Modern Art, New York. Purchase

25

15. *Pablo Picasso*
LADY IN A STRAW HAT. Juan-les-Pins,
May 1, 1936
Oil on canvas, 24 × 19 ¾" (61 × 50 cm)
Musée Picasso, Paris

sculptures, photographs, and documents that have come to light in the various corners of his bequest. At the same time, the work of John Richardson, aided by Marilyn McCully, is now yielding a monumental new biography of the artist, with its first two volumes revealing much that had been unknown about the artist's youth and maturation. At the twentieth century's end, with all this new ammunition, familiar battles over interpretation and evaluation have been rekindled, and our idea of Picasso—far from solidifying into historical certainty—seems to be at least as rapidly evolving, as prone to contention, and as open to change as it has been at any point since he first emerged to change the course of art in our time.

Notes

1. Max Jacob, "Souvenirs sur Picasso contés par Max Jacob," *Cahiers d'Art*, no. 6 (1927), p. 199; translated in Marilyn McCully, ed., *A Picasso Anthology: Documents, Criticism, Reminiscences* (Princeton, N.J.: Princeton University Press, 1982), p. 37.

2. See Edward F. Fry, *Cubism* (New York: McGraw-Hill, 1966; reprinted 1978); McCully, ed., *A Picasso Anthology*, pp. 69–101; Linda Dalrymple Henderson, *The Fourth Dimension and Non-Euclidean Geometry in Modern Art* (Princeton, N.J.: Princeton University Press, 1983); and Henderson, "X Rays and the Quest for Invisibility in the Art of Kupka,

Duchamp, and the Cubists," *Art Journal* 47, no. 4 (Winter 1988), pp. 323–40.

3. Robert Rosenblum, "Picasso and the Typography of Cubism," in Roland Penrose and John Golding, eds., *Picasso in Retrospect* (New York: Praeger, 1973), pp. 49–75.

4. See, for example, David Cottington, "What the Papers Say: Politics and Ideology in Picasso's Collages of 1912," *Art Journal* 47, no. 4 (Winter 1988), pp. 350–59; and Patricia Leighten, *Re-ordering the Universe: Picasso and Anarchism, 1897–1914* (Princeton, N.J.: Princeton University Press, 1989).

5. See Robert Rosenblum, "Picasso and the Anatomy of Eroticism," in Theodore Bowie and Cornelia V. Christenson, eds., *Studies in Erotic Art* (New York: Basic Books, 1970), pp. 337–50 (reprinted in Gert Schiff, ed., *Picasso in Perspective* [Englewood Cliffs, N.J.: Prentice-Hall, 1976], pp. 75–85); Rosalind Krauss, "In the Name of Picasso," *October*, no. 16 (Spring 1981), pp. 5–22 (reprinted in *The Originality of the Avant-garde and Other Modernist Myths* [Cambridge, Mass.: MIT Press, 1985], pp. 23–40).

6. Leo Steinberg, "The Philosophical Brothel," *ARTnews* 71, no. 5 (September 1972), pp. 20–29, and no. 6 (October 1972), pp. 38–47; reprinted in *October* 44 (Spring 1988), pp. 7–74.

7. See Judith Cousins, with Pierre Daix, "Documentary Chronology," in William Rubin, *Picasso and Braque: Pioneering Cubism* (New York: The Museum of Modern Art, 1989), p. 348.

8. Leo Stein, *Appreciation: Painting, Poetry and Prose* (New York: Crown, 1947), pp. 168–88.

9. See, for instance, Benjamin H.D. Buchloh, "Figures of Authority, Ciphers of Regression," in Buchloh, Serge Guilbaut, and David Solkin, eds., *Modernism and Modernity: The Vancouver Conference Papers* (Halifax: The Press of the Nova Scotia College of Art and Design, 1983), pp. 84, 86; and Adam Gopnik, "Escaping Picasso," *The New Yorker*, December 16, 1996, p. 97.

10. Contrast Henry McBride, "Picasso's Guernica," *The New York Sun*, May 6, 1939 (reprinted in Daniel Catton Rich, ed., *The Flow of Art: Essays and Criticism of Henry McBride* [New York: Atheneum, 1975], pp. 367–68); Clement Greenberg, "Picasso Since 1945," *Artforum* 5, no. 2 (October 1966), pp. 28–31 (reprinted in John O'Brian, ed., *Clement Greenberg: The Collected Essays and Criticism, Volume 4: Modernism with a Vengeance, 1957–1969* [Chicago and London: The University of Chicago Press, 1993], p. 236); and Gopnik, "Escaping Picasso," p. 98.

11. See Jeffrey S. Weiss, *The Popular Culture of Modern Art: Picasso, Duchamp, and Avant-gardism* (New Haven, Conn.: Yale University Press, 1994), pp. 1–47.

12. See Fernande Olivier, *Picasso and His Friends* (New York: Appleton-Century, 1965), p. 84; and Pierre Daix, *Picasso: Life and Art* (New York: HarperCollins/Icon Editions, 1993), pp. 63–64.

13. See Daix, *Picasso: Life and Art*, pp. 63–64; and John Richardson, with the collaboration of Marilyn McCully, *A Life of Picasso, Volume I: 1881–1906* (New York: Random House, 1991), p. 417.

14. Daix, *Picasso: Life and Art*, p. 323.

15. The earliest version of this maxim seems to appear in Picasso's 1923 statement to Marius de Zayas: "In my opinion to search means nothing in painting. To find, is the thing" (Marius de Zayas, "Picasso Speaks," *The Arts* 3, no. 5 [May 1923], p. 62; reprinted in Alfred H. Barr, Jr., *Picasso: Fifty Years of His Art* [New York: The Museum of Modern Art, 1946], p. 270).

16. See Sydney Picasso, Robert Rosenblum, et al., *Picasso: A Contemporary Dialogue* (Salzburg and Paris: Galerie Thaddeus Ropac, 1996); and Rosenblum, *Andy Warhol: Heads (after Picasso)* (Paris and Salzburg: Galerie Thaddeus Ropac, 1997).

16. *Jasper Johns*
UNTITLED. 1986
Charcoal and pastel on paper, 29¾ × 42"
(75.6 × 106.7 cm)
The Museum of Modern Art, New York.
Fractional gift of Agnes Gund

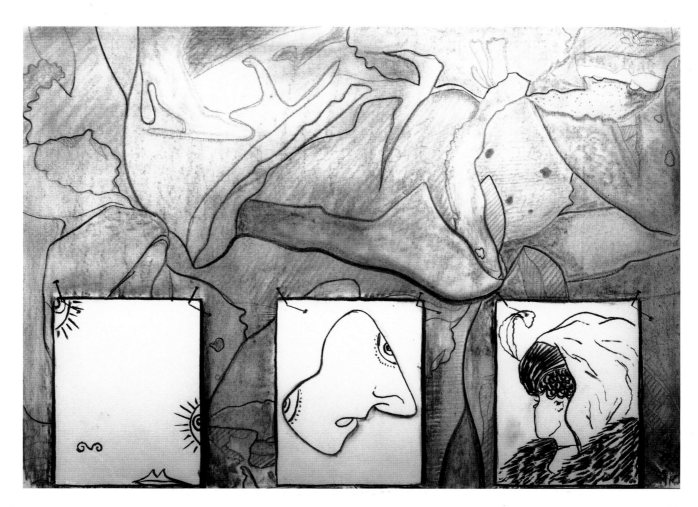

Picasso working on **PREGNANT WOMAN**
(plate, p. 127), c. 1950
Photograph by Edward Quinn

CHRONOLOGY

1881 Pablo Ruiz Picasso is born October 25, 1881, in Málaga, Spain. The first child of María Picasso y Lopez and José Ruiz Blasco, a painter and art teacher, he demonstrates notable artistic talent before the age of ten.

1895 Picasso's father is appointed to the School of Fine Arts in Barcelona; Picasso is immediately admitted to advanced classes there.

1899 Joins the avant-garde circle of Els Quatre Gats, a Barcelona café.

1900 Makes his first trip to Paris, returning to Barcelona after two months.

1901 On his second trip to Paris, Picasso's brightly-colored canvases are exhibited by Ambroise Vollard, Paul Cézanne's dealer. Later that year, Picasso shifts to the monochrome palette of the Blue Period.

1904 After alternating between Barcelona and Paris, Picasso settles definitively in the French capital, taking a studio at 13, rue Ravignan, a ramshackle structure in the heart of Montmartre known as the Bateau-Lavoir ("laundry barge"). That fall, he meets Fernande Olivier, an artist's model who will be his companion for the next seven years. Picasso shifts to the softer palette and classical forms of the Rose Period toward the end of the year.

1905 Leo and Gertrude Stein, American expatriates who have been collecting the works of Cézanne and Henri Matisse, begin to buy his paintings.

1907 Picasso paints *Les Demoiselles d'Avignon;* its radically simplified forms and aggressive sexuality shock even his friends and supporters.

1908 The interlocking geometric shapes of the *Three Women* (now in the Hermitage Museum, St. Petersburg) announce the beginnings of Cubism. Picasso challenges Matisse for leadership of the Parisian avant-garde.

1910–14 Working closely with Georges Braque (formerly a Matisse follower), Picasso invents the revolutionary styles of Analytic and Synthetic Cubism, and the new mediums of collage and constructed sculpture.

1912 Picasso's new companion, Éva Gouel, initiates an era of domestic contentment. They move from Montmartre to 242, boulevard Raspail, in Montparnasse. After the outbreak of war in the summer of 1914, friends like Braque and the poet Guillaume Apollinaire leave for military service, and Éva dies after a long illness in December 1915.

1916 The poet Jean Cocteau persuades Picasso to collaborate on the Ballets Russes production of *Parade,* with music by Erik Satie. The ballet's opening in May 1917 provokes a scandal in wartime Paris.

1918 Picasso marries Olga Khokhlova, a dancer from the Ballets Russes, and moves to the fashionable rue La Boëtie. Seemingly abandoning the art world for high society, he collaborates on a series of ballets, including *Le Tricorne* (1919), *Pulcinella* (1920), *Cuadro Flamenco* (1921), and *Mercure* (1924). In his painting, he alternates between a neoclassical, realist style and a flattened, decorative Cubism.

1920 Picasso and Olga begin summering regularly on the Atlantic coast or on the

Riviera (until then a winter resort). Their son, Paulo, is born in 1921. Images of bathers and mothers and sons assume a prominent place in his work.

1925 Losing interest in ballet and high society, Picasso paints his savage *Dance* in June 1925 (Tate Gallery, London). It is reproduced in the July issue of *La Révolution surréaliste (The Surrealist Revolution)*, where the movement's leader, André Breton, declares that Surrealism can find its path "simply by going where Picasso has gone and will go."

1926 As his marriage founders, Picasso begins an affair with a young woman, Marie-Thérèse Walter, whose face and initials slowly begin to infiltrate his art, which is simultaneously haunted by monstrous images of his wife Olga.

1928 With the collaboration of Julio Gonzalez, Picasso creates a series of welded-metal constructions, launching a new revolution in modern sculpture.

1930 Buys the château of Boisgeloup, near Paris. In 1931, he converts the stables into a sculpture studio where he executes a series of plaster heads of Marie-Thérèse. In his paintings of early 1932, she emerges as a triumphant symbol of erotic bliss.

1932 A large retrospective shown at the Galerie Georges Petit, Paris, and the Zurich Kunsthaus is greeted with largely negative criticism, culminating in an essay by the psychoanalyst Carl Jung diagnosing Picasso's art as schizophrenic.

1935 Marie-Thérèse and Picasso have a daughter, Maya.

1936 Picasso declares his support for the newly-elected Popular Front in France and for the Republican government in Spain, under attack by Francisco Franco's right-wing forces. He is named honorary director of the Prado Museum in Madrid.

1937 Picasso paints the twenty-six-foot canvas *Guernica,* protesting the destruction of the Spanish town by Nazi bombers. The picture's evolution is recorded by his new companion, Dora Maar, a Surrealist photographer who frequently appears as a weeping woman in his paintings of the late 1930s.

1939 After the German invasion of Poland, Picasso moves his multiple households to the port of Royan, on the Atlantic Coast. When the Germans reach Royan in 1940, he returns to Paris, spending the remainder of the war years in his studio on the rue des Grands-Augustins.

1944 After the liberation of Paris, Picasso joins the Communist Party, which has taken a leading role in the French Resistance.

1946 Picasso begins living with Françoise Gilot, a young painter he had met during the war. Their son Claude is born in 1947, their daughter Paloma in 1949. Picasso executes numerous ceramics in the southern town of Vallauris, and makes sculptures incorporating pots and other found objects.

1953 Françoise leaves Picasso, and he meets Jacqueline Roque, the Sphinx-like muse of his late work, whom he marries in 1961. They occupy a series of villas in the South of France, filled with the accumulated masterpieces of a lifetime, and with a never-ending stream of new paintings, drawings, and prints.

1973 Picasso dies on April 8, 1973, at the age of ninety-one.

PICASSO

Masterworks from The Museum of Modern Art

Meditation (Contemplation). *Paris, late 1904*

This large watercolor records an important moment from Picasso's early life, and also announces a theme—the sleeper observed—that would fascinate him recurrently through the years. The time is late 1904, when the artist settled definitively in Paris after a period of restless shuttling back and forth to Spain, and began a new phase in his art. Since the suicide of his friend the poet Carlos Casagemas in 1901, Picasso had focused, in a mournful palette of blues and grays, on the pathos of the infirm and the impoverished. Now, as this work already suggests, his themes would embrace a more poignant tenderness, as his palette shifted to lighter, rosier tones. At least a part of this shift may owe to the changed circumstances of Picasso's life, and particularly to the advent of his first long-term love affair, with Fernande Olivier. The drawing, which shows Picasso and Fernande in the cozy togetherness of a first *ménage*, also poses an opposition between their two states of consciousness—the shadowy realm of upright observation, set beside the luminous glow of recumbent slumber. Picasso preferred to paint late into the night, and thus must often have found himself awake while his lover slept. From the seed of this personal experience, he constructed an emblematic formula with broader ramifications: waking consciousness versus the dream state, attentive looking versus reverie. Picasso's depiction of himself lost in rapt and silent contemplation stresses not only his bewitchment by feminine beauty, but also his deep wonder at the power of the unconscious mind, the state of imagination loosed from humdrum daily perception in the fantasy world of the dreamer. K.V.

MEDITATION (CONTEMPLATION). Paris, late 1904
Watercolor and pen and ink on paper, 14½ × 10½"
(36.9 × 26.7 cm). Zervos I, 235. D.B. XI, 12
Louise Reinhardt Smith Bequest

The Frugal Repast. *Paris, September 1904*

Fernande Olivier, who met Picasso while he was working on this etching, described its subject as "a wretched, starving couple . . . sitting at a table in a wine-shop." Indeed, most critics have seen the couple as victims of urban poverty, injured, love-less, and demoralized. The etching's composition seems to derive from that of a 1903 painting by Picasso, *The Blind Man's Meal* (The Metropolitan Museum of Art, New York). In the painting, the blind man faces left, reaching across a crumpled napkin to touch a jug of wine and a crust of bread. In the etching, the scene has been rotated ninety degrees counter-clockwise, so that the objects on the table separate the figure from the viewer. The empty bowl in the foreground echoes the cavities of the man's eyeless sockets, and he turns his face away, as if refusing the pretense of eye-to-eye contact; but his preternaturally long fingers reach out to grasp his companion's arm and shoulder. The gaunt features and elongated limbs of both figures reflect Picasso's study of Gothic sculpture and Mannerist painting, especially the then recently rediscovered canvases of El Greco. The woman's pendulous breasts recall those of the hunched-over woman in Vincent van Gogh's 1882 lithograph *Sorrow,* but her proudly raised shoulders and coolly speculative gaze reject any hint of self-pity. Even the blind man, with his bowler hat and tousled neck scarf, evinces a kind of threadbare elegance. The earliest impressions of this etching (such as the one reproduced here) were printed for Picasso by August Delâtre, who had previously worked with Camille Corot and Édouard Manet, and was renowned for producing heavily inked, atmospheric images. Picasso subsequently sold the plate to the dealer Ambroise Vollard, who had it steel-faced and reprinted by Louis Fort in a noticeably drier, more linear style.   P.K.

THE FRUGAL REPAST (LE REPAS FRUGAL),
state II. Paris, September 1904
Etching, plate: 18 3/16 × 14 7/8" (46.2 × 37.8 cm).
Geiser/Baer I, 2. Gift of Thomas T. Solley with
Mary Ellen Meehan, and purchase through the
Vincent d'Aquila and Harry Soviak Bequest, and
with contributions from Lily Auchincloss, The
Associates Fund, The Philip and Lynn Straus
Foundation, and John S. Newberry (by exchange)

A mi buen amigo
Sbastián Junyent
Picasso
Paris septiembre 1904

The Jester. *Paris, 1905*

The melancholy king with his battered crown and the brooding jester with his pointed cap are almost interchangeable figures in Picasso's work of 1905, often symbolizing friends like Max Jacob and Guillaume Apollinaire. *The Jester* was, in fact, begun as a portrait of Jacob, one evening when he and Picasso had just returned from the circus. Poet, secretary, shop clerk, and occasional art critic, Jacob had sought out Picasso after admiring his 1901 exhibition at the Paris gallery of Ambroise Vollard. For several months in 1902, the two impoverished friends shared a room on the boulevard Voltaire, Picasso sleeping by day while Jacob worked in a department store, Jacob sleeping by night while Picasso drew and painted. In their hours together, Jacob taught Picasso French and inspired him with his love of French poetry. Later, at the Bateau-Lavoir studio on the rue Ravignan, Jacob remained the court jester of Picasso's circle, sometimes declaiming the poems of Charles Baudelaire, Paul Verlaine, and Arthur Rimbaud, sometimes rolling up his trousers for a peasant dance or donning a woman's hat to sing operettas. The 1905 bust began as a realistic portrait but was transformed the next day, when Picasso added the jester's cap and modified the facial features so that only the lower part of the face resembled Jacob. As the realistic resemblance faded, the image became a deeper, more symbolic portrait. The clay original (which Picasso may have fired as a ceramic in the kiln of his friend Paco Durrio) was sold in spring 1910 to Vollard, who had it cast in bronze. The flicker of highlights and shadows over an uneven surface recalls Auguste Rodin, but the work's strongest feature seems ultimately to be the fool's cap, with its drooping peak and its regal points, bending outwards like petals of a flower. P.K.

THE JESTER. Paris, 1905
Bronze (cast 1950s), 15¼ × 13¾ × 8⅝" (38.7 × 34.8 × 21.9 cm). Spies 4. Louise Reinhardt Smith Bequest

The Acrobats. *Paris, 1905*

Three or four nights a week, for months on end, Picasso and Fernande Olivier visited the Cirque Médrano, which had in earlier years attracted artists like Edgar Degas and Georges Seurat. The solitary outcasts of Picasso's 1901–04 work now assumed a new identity as a troupe of circus performers, and the mournful blues of his earlier paintings gave way to a new palette of pink, red, and gray, seemingly inspired by the reddish costumes and sets of the Médrano. As Theodore Reff has shown, the *personae dramatis* of Picasso's new work descended from a long line of harlequins, *saltimbanques,* clowns, and fools, depicted by nineteenth- and early–twentieth-century novelists, poets, painters, and illustrators. But Picasso minimized the theatrical quality of his characters, stressing everyday activities instead. In *The Acrobats,* a man in harlequin costume watches his daughter practice balancing on a ball, while the other members of his family gather kindling, wash dishes, sew, or play with a baby. No one notices as a pot boils and two toddlers fight in the dirt. Picasso's new interest in family life as a subject may have reflected the novel domesticity of his relationship with Fernande, or their friendship with the painter Kees van Dongen and his wife and daughter, who had recently moved into a nearby studio in the Bateau Lavoir. (In her 1933 memoir, *Picasso and His Friends,* Fernande Olivier recalled that "Picasso spent hours playing with the little girl, who always used to call him 'Tablo.'") Spread out in a lateral frieze, the figures in *The Acrobats* retain the elongated, mannerist proportions of the couple in *The Frugal Repast* (plate, p. 35). Rising behind them like a stage flat, the desolate landscape with its two leafless trees could be the Spanish highlands, or the empty zone just beyond the Paris city walls. Picasso's etching served as a model, first for a small gouache and then for an extremely large canvas begun in spring 1905. After seeing Édouard Manet's 1862 *Old Musician* in that year's Salon d'Automne, he completely repainted the canvas as a more formal and hieratic composition of costumed performers confronting, or pointedly ignoring, the viewer's gaze. (The finished picture, now known as *The Family of Saltimbanques,* is in the National Gallery of Art, Washington, D.C.) P.K.

THE ACROBATS (LES SALTIMBANQUES),
state II. Paris, 1905; printed 1913

Drypoint, plate: 11¼ × 12⅞" (28.5 × 32.7 cm).
Geiser/Baer I, 9. Gift of Abby Aldrich Rockefeller

Circus Rider. *Paris, 1905*

One of the secrets of Picasso's astounding productivity was his ability to recycle. He could generate a seemingly endless series of "new" pictures by mixing and matching figures, gestures, and forms taken from old ones. The young girl balancing on a ball at the right of *The Acrobats* (previous page) later became the main subject of a large canvas, *Young Acrobat on a Ball* (now in the Pushkin Museum, Moscow), and then metamorphosed into a circus rider, balancing on a horse instead of a ball, the emaciated child now a robust young woman who confidently masters her cantering steed. Having fixed on this new motif, Picasso experimented with a variety of poses and gestures. The rider is sometimes standing, sometimes seated. Her arms may be raised or lowered, straight or bent. In this delicately tinted sketch, the rider balances on one foot; the horse beneath her is reduced to the outlines of neck, back, and hindquarters. In contrast to the apparent stillness of the rider, the fluttering lines of the horse's mane and tail suggest frenzied motion. In another drawing from this series, the rider is seated, but her pose, with one hand extended and the other cocked on her hip, seems to provide the model for the "laureate gesture" of the standing figure in *Boy Leading a Horse* (plate, p. 43). Picasso's figures of the Rose Period, both male and female, display a haunting combination of fragility and self-assurance. P.K.

CIRCUS RIDER. Paris, 1905
Ink and watercolor on paper: 8 ¼ × 5 ⅛" (22.2 × 13.1 cm). The William S. Paley Collection

Boy Leading a Horse. *Paris, 1905–06*

Picasso's Rose Period began with a residue of late nineteenth-century sentiment and Symbolism, with its pink-tinted imagery of wistfully alienated harlequins and circus performers. In its later phases, however, there is a notable shift from the tender to the tough, with a new palette of sand and terra-cotta, and a marked inflection of sculpturally potent classicism. The circus types who dominate this new imagery, as in the monumental *Family of Saltimbanques,* seem generally less afflicted, more independent, and possessed of a sober dignity. One of the most ambitious projects of this latter phase was *The Watering Place,* a large composition conceived on the theme of men and horses gathered at a stream. Several sketches survive, but the painting was never realized, and this large-scale stele of a rigid youth beside his slender steed was Picasso's distillation of those mural-like ambitions. The motif of the horse tamer, symbolic of human will and civilization mastering unruly animal nature, is at least as ancient as the sculptural frieze of the Parthenon. The actual gesture of this youth, however, had a more mundane and immediate origin, in Picasso's studies of a female acrobatic rider, standing on a horse with her arm outstretched for balance. In the way Picasso uses the gesture here, especially with the elimination of any indication of reins, the notion of mastery through the dominance of mind rather than through physical struggle is made all the more insistent: the boy's clenched fist and extended arm seem to control the animal by unseen magic. The evident influence of archaic Greek sculpture on the figure's pose and physique represents one of the first instances of Picasso's lifelong fascination with the art and culture of Mediterranean antiquity. It mingles here with the early indices, in the modeling of the body, of his crucial engagement with the art of Paul Cézanne. The embrace of these new influences, the scale of the picture, its theme of mastery, the youthful rectitude of the boy—all these announce a new assertiveness and self-confidence in Picasso's approach to his art. K.V.

BOY LEADING A HORSE. Paris, 1905–06
Oil on canvas, 7'2⅞" × 57⅝" (220.6 × 131.2 cm).
Zervos I, 264. D.B. XIV, 7
The William S. Paley Collection. 575.64

Two Nudes. *Paris, late 1906*

From 1901 through 1908, Picasso returned almost obsessively to the image of two women standing face-to-face or side-by-side. A 1902 painting of this motif (*The Visit [Two Sisters]*; Hermitage Museum, St. Petersburg) seems to depict a nun consoling a diseased prostitute. In contrast, Picasso refrained from moralizing in this 1906 picture: the women's beckoning gestures invite the viewer to part the curtains and enter. The challenging stare of the woman on the left recalls Édouard Manet's 1863 *Olympia,* exhibited at the Salon d'Automne of 1905. In his earlier depictions of pairs of women, Picasso had drawn on stylistic models ranging from antique gravestones to Gothic sculpture. The arched brows, exaggerated eyelids and oversized ears of the *Two Nudes* reflect a new influence, that of Iberian sculpture. Several recently discovered examples, displayed at the Louvre in spring 1906, demonstrates that a powerful "primitive" style could re-emerge within the sophisticated conventions of classical art—a lesson clearly not lost on Picasso. There is no antecedent in Iberian sculpture, however, for the bulky bodies and stumpy legs of the *Two Nudes*. These may be meant to express the underlying masculine character that late nineteenth-century science attributed to prostitutes. But the figures' proportions are most closely anticipated in several drawings of young boys and girls from the summer of 1906: in effect, they are children who have blossomed too quickly into sexual maturity. P.K.

TWO NUDES. Paris, late 1906
Oil on canvas, 59⅝ × 36⅝" (151.3 × 93 cm)
Zervos I, 366. D.B. XVI, 15. Gift of G. David Thompson in honor of Alfred H. Barr, Jr.

Head of a Sleeping Woman. *Paris, summer 1907*

After arriving at the massive sculptural forms of the *Two Nudes* (plate, p. 45), Picasso embarked in 1907 on an agonizing reappraisal of what his dealer and friend Daniel-Henry Kahnweiler called "the basic tasks of painting: to represent three dimensions and color on a flat surface, and to comprehend them in the unity of that surface." Picasso began by reducing his figures to combinations of curves and angles—sometimes seen in isolation, sometimes linked together by lines suggesting drapery. This simplification and flattening of individual forms seems to have been inspired by sources ranging from archaic Greek vases to the most recent paintings by Henri Matisse, while the dovetailing of these forms into rhythmic patterns of interlocking curves reflects the influences of Romanesque sculpture and art nouveau ironwork. Picasso did not need to leave Paris in order to study the swaying figures and criss-crossing draperies of Romanesque statuary; plaster casts of masterpieces from Vézelay, Souillac, and Chartres were conveniently collected in the Museum of Comparative Sculpture, which occupied (and still occupies) the left wing of the Palais de Trocadéro. "One day, as he was leaving," Christian Zervos recounted, "a curious impulse moved him to open the door across the hall, which led to the rooms of what was then known as the Museum of Ethnography." Years later, Zervos recalled, "Picasso spoke with profound emotion of the African sculptures he saw there and the shock they gave him." As William Rubin has argued, what Picasso took away from this encounter was a new sense of the magical power of art, and in particular of the expressive value of the rhythmic incisions found on certain African sculptures. These were transcribed into his new paintings as slashing hatch marks, like those that cover the *Head of a Sleeping Woman*, modulating from black, brown, red, and green in her face to green and tan in the drapery at right. Kahnweiler wrote that Picasso "placed sharp-edged images on the canvas, heads and nudes mostly, in the brightest colors: yellow, red, blue and black. He applied the colors in thread-like fashion to serve as lines of direction, and to build up, in conjunction with the drawing, the plastic effect." The Kota reliquary figures that impressed Picasso may also have influenced the pose of the figure in the larger canvas *Nude with Drapery* (1907; Hermitage Museum, St. Petersburg), for which the *Head of a Sleeping Woman* is a study. P.K.

HEAD OF A SLEEPING WOMAN (Study for NUDE WITH DRAPERY). Paris, summer 1907
Oil on canvas, 24¼ × 18¾" (61.4 × 47.6 cm)
Zervos II*, 44. D.R. 93. Estate of John Hay Whitney

Fruit Dish. *Paris, winter 1908–09*

Following his fierce engagement with tribal art and with emotionally-charged figural subjects in 1907, Picasso's art came under the sway of two calming or disciplining influences, from the widely different paintings of Henri Rousseau and Paul Cézanne. Focusing on the more objective motif of the still life, Picasso painted several canvases—including this severe composition of greens and ochers—that attempt to synthesize the lessons of these so disparate artists. With its central fruit dish set against a large gourd and swag of drapery on an uptilted tabletop, this picture owes an evident debt to the sophisticated still lifes of Cézanne. The rhythmically structured passages of parallel brushstrokes reflect the same source. The overall coloration, however, as well as the more straightforward sculptural modeling of light and dark, and especially the emphasis on sharply defined contours, seem to stem from Rousseau—perhaps particularly from the painstakingly verdant landscapes of hallucinatory jungles that were central to Picasso's fascination with Rousseau's seemingly self-taught, naive manner. Among the other still lifes of the same period, this one is distinguished by its sinuous linear energies. The Cézanne-inspired rendering of the drape and table is angular and faceted, but the scalloped edge of the dish, the clustered fruits, and the gourd with its climbing stem all writhe with a curvilinear pulse more characteristic of the decorative organic flourishes of late-nineteenth-century art nouveau. K.V.

FRUIT DISH. Paris, winter 1908–09
Oil on canvas, 29 ¼ × 24" (74.3 × 61 cm)
Zervos II*, 121. D.R. 210
Acquired through the Lillie P. Bliss Bequest

Bather. *Paris, 1908–09*

Picasso's *Bather* looks back toward the *contraposto* nudes of academic tradition, and forward toward the multiple viewpoints of Analytic Cubism. Breasts and back, pubis and buttocks—all are simultaneously visible. As Leo Steinberg has argued, Picasso's lifelong obsession with depicting the female body from all directions at once seems to have derived from an almost magical belief that to draw a figure was to possess it. The figure's placement on a featureless beach beside a waveless sea, beneath an empty sky, may have been inspired—as John Richardson has suggested—by Henri Matisse's 1908 paintings of nude bathers on abstract shores. Some of Picasso's studies echo the linear outlines of Matisse's bathers. But Picasso diverged from his rival by doubling the contour of the back and buttocks, giving the impression that the figure is constructed from flattened, overlapping planes—an idea that would bear fruit in 1913 pictures like the *Card Player* (plate, p. 71). Other, related drawings depict figures constructed from interlacing strands, outlining the contours of the body without filling in the spaces between them—a sculptural idea that Picasso finally realized in the *Monument to Guillaume Apollinaire* of 1928 (plate, p. 95). The *Bather*'s pose, with one arm raised to her brow, may have been suggested by J.-A.-D. Ingres, the neoclassical master whose elongated nudes, exhibited at the 1905 Salon d'Automne, would also have provided poetic license for Picasso's willful distortions of anatomy. But the graceful curves and porcelain skin of Ingres's nudes are replaced in the *Bather* by tight-sprung contours and hatched shading that make it look like one of the "flayed" figures traditionally used to teach artists about the body's hidden musculature. P.K.

BATHER. Paris, 1908–09
Oil on canvas, sight 51 × 38⅛" (130 × 96.5 cm)
Zervos II*, 111. D.R. 239
Louise Reinhardt Smith Bequest

Head. *Paris, spring 1909*

In spring 1908, Picasso painted a series of pictures representing the human head as a geometric solid, its features reduced to flat or gently curving planes. He returned to this idea in the spring and summer of 1909, executing numerous drawings and paintings of Fernande Olivier with her hair put up in a geometrical bun, and her face divided into gemlike facets. The goal of this faceting, he told Kahnweiler, was to achieve a more exact representation of the human head: "It seemed to Picasso that not only the Impressionists but all Western painters had lacked precision in the figuration of volume. He often commented on this topic. 'In a head by Raphael,' he one day said to me, 'it is impossible to measure with exactness the distance between the mouth and the end of the nose. I would like it to be possible to measure this in my paintings.'" But the appearance of precision in Picasso's 1909 work is often deceptive. When the multiplication of planes began to generate confusion instead of clarity, he simplified the composition by merging neighboring facets, creating new forms that sometimes bear only a tangential relationship to the actual anatomy of the human face. Discussing this *Head* of spring 1909, Alfred H. Barr, Jr., commented on "the bold elision which includes the far side of the nose and cheek in one plane extending to the right *beyond* the receding curve of the brow." As Barr noted, this elision anticipates the even bolder treatment of the head in Picasso's 1910 *Girl with a Mandolin (Fanny Tellier)* (plate, p. 59), where the entire right side of the face is reduced to a single featureless plane. The merging of forms in the 1909 *Head* seems to recall Paul Cézanne's technique (known as *passage*) of using continuous brushwork to link adjacent motifs. Picasso's long narrow strokes of gray, brown, tan, and black, marking the spatial orientation of each plane, can also be seen as allusions to Cézanne's rhythmic brushstrokes. From other studies in this series, it is evident that Fernande posed with her head tilted back, leaning against her raised right arm. Positioning himself slightly below her, Picasso exposed the planes below brow and chin that are usually hidden in portrait drawings, giving the impression that her face looms up above the viewer, as monumental as an Easter Island head or an overhanging cliff. P.K.

HEAD. Paris, spring 1909
Gouache on paper, 24½ × 18⅞" (62.2 × 48 cm)
Zervos II*, 148. D.R. 266. Gift of Saidie A. May

53

Woman's Head (Fernande). *Paris, fall 1909*

Picasso spent the summer of 1909 in the small Spanish town of Horta de Ebro, where he executed a series of drawings and paintings depicting Fernande's face and torso broken into ever-smaller facets. That fall, back in Paris, he sculpted this *Woman's Head*, which seems to translate the summer's paintings from two into three dimensions. Daniel-Henry Kahnweiler and other scholars have seen this head as a logical extension of the "Impressionist" sculptures of Auguste Rodin and Medardo Rosso. With its alternating hollows and projections, the bronze seems to depict not the actual form of the head but the play of light across its surface. Yet the light-catching facets of the *Woman's Head* may not have been part of Picasso's original concept. Rather, his initial idea seems to have been to construct the head from interwoven, freestanding strands like those in the sketches related to the spring 1909 *Bather* (plate, p. 51). "I thought that the curves you see on the surface should continue into the interior," he told Roland Penrose. "I had the idea of doing them in wire." Finding this impractical, Picasso instead decided to model the curves of his design as ridges on the surface of a solid mass. The idea of interweaving solid strands around a hollow volume remains visible in the lower part of the face, where the mass of the head has been deeply excavated around the narrow ridges tracing the contours of mouth and cheeks. There is a disturbing quality to the bronze *Head* and the paintings that precede it, evident in Fernande's strained expression and bloated features. She was, in fact, seriously ill during this period. But Picasso offered a different explanation, cited by Gertrude Stein: "When you make a thing, it is so complicated making it that it is bound to be ugly, but those that do it after you they don't have to worry about making it and they can make it pretty." Indeed, the cutaway view of the *Head*'s facial features exerted an important influence on avant-garde sculptors like Umberto Boccioni and Naum Gabo. Picasso himself returned to the idea of openwork, constructed sculpture in his 1912 *Guitar* (maquette, p. 65) and his 1928 *Project for a Monument to Guillaume Apollinaire* (plates, p. 95). P.K.

WOMAN'S HEAD (FERNANDE). Paris, fall 1909
Bronze, 16¼ × 9¾ × 10½" (41.3 × 24.7 × 26.6 cm)
Spies 24. Purchase

Still Life with Liqueur Bottle. *Horta de Ebro, August 1909*

During the summer at Horta de Ebro, Picasso focused almost exclusively on the human figure and the surrounding landscape. Returning over and over to the same motifs, he evolved a new style, dissolving three-dimensional form into a series of facets shaded with a severely limited palette of green, brown, black, and white. *Still Life with Liqueur Bottle* seems to have been painted to test whether this new style could be applied to a broader range of motifs. The repetition of small planes, unifying foreground and background into a single faceted surface, looks forward toward Analytic Cubist still lifes like *The Architect's Table* of 1912 (plate, p. 61). As in Analytic Cubism, the dissolution of form in the *Still Life with Liqueur Bottle* has been taken to the point where it is difficult to perceive the identity of individual objects. This painting was described for many years as a *Still Life with Syphon*, and then as a *Still Life with Tube of Paint*. Not until 1971, when William Rubin discussed the picture with Picasso, were its contents clearly identified. At center, there is a *botijo* (a ceramic jug in the shape of a cock), whose presence seems to celebrate Picasso's return to his native Spain. At lower left, there is a large bottle of a Spanish liqueur, Anis del Mono, with its distinctive diamond-shaped facets, and a second, smaller liqueur bottle covered with interwoven ridges (perhaps meant to imitate straw). These objects seem to have been chosen both for their Spanish character and because they conformed so effortlessly to Picasso's new pictorial vocabulary. At right appear the more typical Cubist motifs of a glass with a straw and a folded newspaper. Soon after returning to Paris in September 1909, Picasso and Fernande Olivier moved from their squalid quarters in the Bateau-Lavoir to more spacious and elegant lodgings on the boulevard de Clichy. ("These people must have hit the jackpot," exclaimed one of the movers.) The new studio provided the setting for a private exhibition of the summer's paintings. As so often happened, Picasso's latest style proved too challenging for his friends and dealers, and most of his new work (including the *Still Life with Liqueur Bottle*) remained for many years in the artist's possession, unsold. P.K.

STILL LIFE WITH LIQUEUR BOTTLE. Horta de Ebro, August 1909
Oil on canvas, 32⅛ × 25¾" (81.6 × 65.4 cm)
Zervos II*, 173. D.R. 299
Mrs. Simon Guggenheim Fund

Girl with a Mandolin (Fanny Tellier). *Paris, 1910*

During the summer of 1910, Picasso pushed his Cubist stylizations toward a point of near-total abstraction, dissolving solid forms into an open, linear armature of shifting planes. This picture, which was studied (exceptionally) from a posing model, seems by contrast to present an evident dialogue between a shallow architecture of featureless slabs and more traditionally modeled volumes. Scholars have differed as to whether this indicates a transitional work done in the spring, or a work of the autumn in which Picasso began to pull back from the brink of abstraction. Picasso's testimony that Fanny Tellier, the model for this painting, quit prematurely—apparently in protest over the slow progress of the many sessions—adds a further element of doubt. How much further might the painter have elaborated passages like the neck and face, which seem uncharacteristically plain and whole amidst the general fragmentation of forms? The motif of the woman with a musical instrument, set against what appears to be a studio backdrop of canvases stacked against each other, likely derives from similar scenes painted by the nineteenth-century artist J.-B.-C. Corot, which Picasso could have seen in an exhibition in fall 1909. Picasso was drawn to these images of a female model contemplating a work of art in the studio setting, and variations on the theme would recur throughout his career (see p. 103). Corot's atmospherics have been overturned here, though, in favor of a Cubist insistence on a gridlike organizing lattice that governs the geometricized facets of both the body and its surroundings. Later works would go much further with the formal puns and analogies that could link mandolins, violins, and guitars to the female body; such stringed instruments would become central, recurring emblems of Cubism. Their presence, here and elsewhere, underlines the strange paradox by which such a radically transforming revolution in art could be realized in terms of the traditional themes and intimate atmosphere of the studio portrait and still life—an explosive cataclysm of representation set forth, in tender chiaroscuro, with the contemplative air of chamber music. K.V.

GIRL WITH A MANDOLIN (FANNY TELLIER).
Paris, 1910
Oil on canvas, 39½ × 29" (100.3 × 73.6 cm)
Zervos II*, 235. D.R. 346
Nelson A. Rockefeller Bequest

The Architect's Table. *Paris, early 1912*

Discussing this picture with William Rubin, Picasso insisted: "All its forms can't be rationalized. At the time, everyone talked about how much reality there was in Cubism. But they didn't really understand. It's not a reality you can take in your hand. It's more like a perfume—in front of you, behind you, to the sides. The scent is everywhere, but you don't quite know where it comes from." This mysterious and indefinite realism emerges only in Picasso's work of winter 1911–12. Recently uncovered archival evidence suggests that the first version of *The Architect's Table*, painted in spring 1911, offered a more prosaic horizontal image of a mandolin and absinthe glass resting on a table covered with a fringed cloth. As in the 1910 *Girl with a Mandolin (Fanny Tellier)* (previous page), the motifs were fractured into a series of geometric contours and glimmering planes, merging with the surrounding space; yet the underlying arrangement still resembled a conventional still life, drawn in perspective. Early in 1912, Picasso returned to the oval canvas, rotating it to a vertical orientation and repainting it almost completely. The mandolin became a vertical violin, the scroll of its neck visible at upper right. Picasso added an absinthe glass at upper left, and a wineglass and a bottle of marc at center. An architect's ruler slopes behind the transparent absinthe glass. On the left, a pipe rests on a piece of sheet music with the inscription *Ma Jolie* ("my pretty one"). The fringed tablecloth was repainted at the bottom. While the painting was still in process, Gertrude Stein stopped at the studio, leaving her calling card since Picasso was out: when he returned, he added it to the composition at lower right. The objects in the revised painting no longer occupy a single, unified space. Their images jostle and overlap, held together not by perspective but by the light and dark strips that weave throughout the composition. They allude to a series of different events: the violin to a J.-A.-D. Ingres retrospective held at the Galeries George Petit in spring 1911 (where the artist's violin—his favorite pastime—had been displayed along with his paintings and drawings); the inscription "ma jolie" to Picasso's newly begun (and still clandestine) affair with Eva Gouel (Marcelle Humbert); and the calling card to Stein's visit. It is worth noting that Stein and her brother Leo, Picasso's most important early patrons, had not bought any of his paintings since 1910, when he shifted decisively into the style of Analytic Cubism. The gallant gesture of reproducing Gertrude's calling card finally persuaded her to buy one of his new pictures. The original version of the canvas had been consigned to the dealer Daniel-Henry Kahnweiler under the title *The Architect-Musician*; after the painting was reworked, this was revised to *The Architect's Table*. But in his letters to Gertrude, Picasso referred to it simply as "your still life *Ma Jolie*." P.K.

THE ARCHITECT'S TABLE. Paris, early 1912
Oil on canvas, mounted on oval panel, 28⅝ × 23½" (72.6 × 59.7 cm). Zervos II*, 321. D.R. 456 The William S. Paley Collection

Standing Nude. *1912*

Picasso's long and stormy relationship with Fernande Olivier came to an end in spring 1912, when she discovered his secret affair with Eva Gouel, the mysterious "pretty one" of *The Architect's Table* (previous page) and other recent paintings. Picasso and his new paramour fled Paris for Céret, a town in southwestern France, where Picasso had enjoyed an idyllic sojourn in summer 1911. After learning that Fernande was planning to follow them there, Picasso and Eva took flight once again, finally settling near Avignon, in Provence. Picasso always idealized Eva, who died, tragically young, in December 1915. Although he executed no realistic portraits of her in 1912, her presence haunts his work, primarily in the form of verbal allusions (*Ma Jolie, J'aime Éva*), but also in a series of nude figure studies more sensual than anything he had done in several years. Looking back to figures like the spring 1909 *Bather* (plate, p. 51), the *Standing Nude*, probably done in summer 1912, turns in mid-stride to expose both breasts and buttocks, their generous curves emerging from a flux of angular planes. Such drawings represent the last hurrah of Analytic Cubism: space itself seems to solidify into rectangular sheets of light and shade, overlapping and intersecting the human figure. But the multiple sign languages of Synthetic Cubism are already taking shape. The figure's breasts are indicated both by shaded curves and by dowel-like cylinders. These seem to have been inspired by the cylindrical eyes of an African mask owned by Picasso, which a few months later provided the model for the projecting sounding hole of his revolutionary *Guitar* (plate, p. 65). In other summer 1912 drawings, a spiral rather than a cylinder serves to represent both breast and sounding hole. In effect, the figure has been reduced to a mix-and-match arrangement of graphic signs. Soon, in works like the *Man with a Hat* (plate, p. 67), Picasso would strip away the veil of overlapping planes and leave these signs bare. In Daniel-Henry Kahnweiler's words, the artist had come to see painting and sculpture as "forms of *writing*. The products of these arts are signs and emblems, and not a mirror, more or less faithful, of the external world." Taking Kahnweiler's argument a step further, scholars have argued that the signs in Picasso's 1912–13 work are fundamentally arbitrary— that is, unrelated to the real forms they represent. Picasso himself stated that "nature . . . is only translatable into painting by signs." "But," he added, "such signs are not invented. To arrive at the sign, you have to concentrate hard on the resemblance." P.K.

STANDING NUDE. 1912
Pen and ink and pencil on paper, 12⅛ × 7⅜"
(30.7 × 18.7 cm). Zervos XXVIII, 38
Louise Reinhardt Smith Bequest

Maquette for **Guitar.** *Paris, October 1912*

The three-dimensional objects Picasso made from 1912 to about 1917 introduced revolutionary new notions of what the methods, forms, and themes of modern sculpture might be. Working often on a modest scale, in unorthodox, humble materials such as wood, paper, and sheet metal, he concocted a wide array of constructions, many involving painted surfaces and collaged elements, dealing with tabletop café still-life themes—glasses, bottles, musical instruments, and items of food. Many of these often ragtag, heterogeneously playful fabrications have only come to light with the emptying of the artist's studio following his death, but the relatively austere *Guitar*, first realized in this paper version and later (in spring 1913) rendered in sheet metal, has long been recognized as a milestone in the renovation of the medium. Stepping outside the subject of the human body that had so dominated Western sculpture, this work also explodes the traditional integral wholeness of sculptural form, and replaces it with a layered assemblage of planes. Moreover, just as solid parts of the guitar are opened up as voids, the central receding void—the sounding hole—is represented by a protruding tube. For that inversion, as well as for the general idea of a work built outward from a supporting plane, Picasso seems to have found encouragement in an African mask he owned, where the eyes stood forward as cylinders from a flat board denoting the head's volume. This paper *Guitar* never had a base; originally part of a larger assemblage that included flat elements suggesting a table and a bottle, it was made to hang on a wall, as real guitars often did in the artist's studio. In this and other respects, Picasso's constructions of the 1910s can seem both pictorial and sculptural, and there has been a great deal of speculation about the relation between these objects— particularly the seminal *Guitar*—and the pictures he assembled from cutout shapes and collaged elements around the same time. Picasso's partner in Cubist experimentation, Georges Braque, had begun making small paper constructions before Picasso, and it now seems clear that Picasso made this paper version of the *Guitar* in the autumn of 1912, just before he began making *papiers collés*. But the idea of sculptural planes suspended in space seems to have concerned Picasso in much earlier drawings, stemming from the opening-up of forms, and radically geometricized abstractions, in his paintings of 1910 and after. K.V.

Maquette for GUITAR. Paris, October 1912
*Construction of cardboard, string, and wire
(restored), 25¾ × 13 × 7½" (65.1 × 33 × 19 cm)
Spies 27A. Gift of the artist*

Man with a Hat. *Paris, December 1912*

In the second half of 1912, the shimmering, overlapping planes of Analytic Cubism suddenly vanished from Picasso's work. The densely interwoven strips of his winter 1911–12 paintings (see, for example, p. 61) survive as a bare scaffolding of vertical and horizontal lines. Faces or objects are suggested by the insertion of a few simple "graphic signs." But apparently simple works like *Man with a Hat* often conceal a long and complex process of composition. Picasso's depiction of the face as a pair of rectangles overlapping an upside-down cone had been worked out in a series of drawings begun in summer 1912. The double curve at left, forming a backwards *B* suggesting the man's brow and cheek, was not originally part of the face, but was imported from his fall 1912 *Guitar* (maquette, previous page). The repetition of the same trapezoidal form at either side of the face challenges the conventional assumption that the human body is symmetrical. On the left, the diagonal side of the trapezoid represents the bridge of the man's nose; on the right, it represents his cheekbone. The two sides are different even if they look exactly alike. The incorporation of pasted elements like newsprint and colored paper was also revolutionary. In spring 1912, Picasso had glued a piece of printed oilcloth onto one of his paintings, initiating the modern practice of collage. Georges Braque, his collaborator in the invention of Cubism, responded by gluing strips of wood-grained wallpaper onto his drawings, inventing the *papier collé*. The poet Guillaume Apollinaire, a friend of Picasso, hastened to find historical precedents for these innovations: "Mosaicists paint with pieces of marble or colored wood. Mention has been made of an Italian painter who painted with fecal matter; at the time of the French Revolution, someone who painted with blood." Breaking down the barrier between art and life, collage posed an unprecedented challenge to painting's status as "high" art. P.K.

MAN WITH A HAT. Paris, December 1912
Cut-and-pasted papers, charcoal, and brush and ink on paper, 24½ × 18⅝" (62.2 × 47.3 cm)
Zervos II**, 398. D.R. 534. Purchase

Glass, Guitar, and Bottle. *Paris, early 1913*

In Analytic Cubist paintings like *The Architect's Table* (plate, p. 61), Picasso had challenged the physical integrity of objects, dissolving them into a welter of overlapping planes. With the emergence of Synthetic Cubism, the things in Picasso's pictures became clearer and more discrete, but the picture itself became a more and more perplexing object. *Glass, Guitar, and Bottle* combines canvas, raised areas of gesso, and pasted strips of paper with oil paint, pencil, and stenciled lettering. Is it a painting, a *papier collé*, or a colored relief? Daniel-Henry Kahnweiler argued that the overlapping planes in Picasso's paintings of this period were imitations of the literal planes found in his relief sculptures, and indeed *Glass, Guitar, and Bottle* reproduces the composition of a relief construction that the artist assembled on the wall of his boulevard Raspail studio in early 1913. Although the construction as a whole no longer exists, a photograph reveals that it incorporated the cardboard maquette for *Guitar* (plate, p. 65), mounted atop a curved piece of dark paper or cardboard representing a tabletop, projecting from the wall at a 60° angle. A drawing of a diamond-patterned bottle (recalling the 1909 *Still Life with Liqueur Bottle* [plate, p. 57]) was pinned to the wall at right; at left, a broad strip of dark paper was folded over to suggest a wainscoted wall with a chair railing. This semiabstract relief seems to have provided the model for a whole series of paintings, drawings, and *papiers collés*, some equally abstract, others containing strikingly realistic glasses and bottles or unanticipated passages of *faux* marble. In *Glass, Guitar, and Bottle*, the curved sides of the cardboard *Guitar* have multiplied into a swarm of larger and smaller *B*-shapes, nestled amid gray and white strips. The cylindrical sounding hole has collapsed into pairs of overlapping circles. Conversely, the *Guitar*'s hollow neck, crossed by frets of string, has been transformed into a row of impastoed ridges whose actual projection is heightened by illusionistic shading. The bottle appears as a white-on-black silhouette at right, while an abstract wineglass at left casts a strangely convincing shadow. When Picasso created this picture, the pictorial vocabulary of *papier collé* was only a few months old, but he could not resist playing tricks with it. The white strips descending from the top of the canvas, seemingly made from cardboard, are in fact built up with gesso. They recall the vertical strips of newsprint in works like *Man with a Hat* (previous page) , but the actual newspapers in *Glass, Guitar, and Bottle* are all glued on horizontally. Compounding the series of "inside" jokes, the cryptic block letters are taken from printed advertisements, but the *RENNES* at upper left (the name of an avenue near Picasso's apartment) has been stenciled on by hand—atop another advertisement. Artifice imitates reality, while reality imitates artifice. P.K.

GLASS, GUITAR, AND BOTTLE. Paris, early 1913

Oil, pasted paper, gesso, and pencil on canvas, 25¾ × 21⅛" (65.4 × 53.6 cm). Zervos II**, 419. D.R. 570 The Sidney and Harriet Janis Collection

69

Card Player. *Paris, winter 1913–14*

Although Picasso's Analytic Cubist paintings of 1910–12 are often highly abstract, their chiaroscuro atmosphere, dappled brushstrokes, and nuanced shadings all belong to the repertoire of traditional art. By contrast, as William Rubin has pointed out, the Synthetic Cubist works painted after 1912—such as this café figure—are both more radically abstract, in their splicing together of disparate flat, cutout shapes that seem to echo *papiers collés*, and more immediately realistic, in their inclusion of passages of varied decorative patterning that refer directly to wood or printed-paper sources. These aspects of collagelike *trompe-l'oeil*, as well as the passages of pointillist stippling and the ballooning, guitarlike curves that suggest the body, connect this work to others made in late 1913 or perhaps early 1914. Despite its high degree of abstraction, the *Card Player* is relatively easy to "decipher": In the midsection we find schemas that represent one arm holding a card faceup (three more are facedown above it), and another holding a pipe, with above them disassembled and remade ears, hair, and an inverted-*T* nose (which derives from an actual typographic *T* Picasso had pasted in as a nose in an earlier collage). In previous painting, from the seventeenth-century Dutch through Paul Cézanne, cardplaying had been predominantly a subject of sociability. Here, however, the figure is isolated, iconic, and rather grave, encouraging the speculation that he may be engaged not merely in solitaire, but in telling fortunes by cards, as did Picasso's close friend the poet Max Jacob. The ace of clubs, which the figure presents, appears frequently in Cubist paintings, and was apparently thought to be a token of good fortune. K.V.

CARD PLAYER. Paris, winter 1913–14
Oil on canvas, 42½ × 35¼" (108 × 89.5 cm)
Zervos II**, 466. D.R. 650
Acquired through the Lillie P. Bliss Bequest

Student with Pipe. *Paris, March 1914*

On March 2, 1914, Picasso's 1905 canvas *The Family of Saltimbanques* was sold at auction for the astonishing price of 11,500 francs, paid by the German dealer Heinrich Thannhauser. In the atmosphere of impending hostilities in Europe, the sale caused a public scandal: German dealers' support for avant-garde artists was seen as a deliberate assault on French culture, and Picasso's more recent work was denounced as a "Cubist bluff." Most of Picasso's paintings and *papiers collés* of spring 1914 are lyrical still lifes, seemingly unrelated to the more literary themes of his pre-Cubist work. But the *Student with Pipe*, along with several contemporary paintings and drawings, reveals a new interest in narrative content. As William Rubin has noted, the beret, made from crumpled paper, is a *faluche* of the type favored by Parisian students, accurate down to the small seal on the headband identifying the student's school. In a related drawing, the same figure wears a plaid vest and plays a guitar. Although everything but the beret is painted, *Student with Pipe* mimics the appearance of *papier collé*. The figure is indicated by lines on a grayish-white ground. The "reverse-*B*" defining the left side of the student's face derives from 1912–13 works like the *Man with a Hat* (plate, p. 67), as does the blue-gray strip behind it. However, the rectilinear framework of the earlier work has dissolved, leaving the overlapping planes and curves of the student's face to tilt tipsily this way and that, deprived of external support. Without the screen of the Cubist grid, the oddness of Picasso's sign language becomes apparent. The absurdly long and narrow nose is formed by a pair of converging lines descending from the eyes, with a blush of pointillist dots suggesting the flush of excessive drinking. The flattened ears stick out like handles at either side of the face. The *Student*'s features provided the starting point for a series of summer 1914 drawings in which Picasso deliberately exaggerated the tension between realistic and geometric elements of his figuration. As Roland Penrose suggested, these "wildly grotesque" drawings were "prophetic of the discoveries of the surrealists, Max Ernst and Miró, ten years later." Surrealism, it might be argued, was the logical extension of Cubism. P.K.

STUDENT WITH PIPE. Paris, March 1914
Gesso, sand, pasted paper, oil, and charcoal on canvas, 28¾ × 23⅛" (73 × 58.7 cm)
Zervos II**, 444. D.R. 620
Nelson A. Rockefeller Bequest

Green Still Life. *Avignon, summer 1914*

The advent, around 1912–13, of Picasso's Synthetic Cubist style, with its flat, seemingly cutout shapes and great variety of decorative textures, blew away the shadowy, Rembrandt-like atmosphere of the Analytic Cubist paintings of 1910–11. Yet at first, the new works were realized with a rather severely limited, dark palette—while other painters influenced by Picasso and Georges Braque's Cubism, such as Robert Delaunay, were already showing pictures where Cubist fragmentation wed bright, rainbow colors. It was only during Picasso's summer stay in Avignon in 1914—in the looming shadow of the coming war, and with his beloved Eva Gouel beset by illness—that his palette began to brighten, and his works took on such cheery hues and polychrome surface decoration that they have sometimes been said to constitute a "rococo" phase of Cubism. *Green Still Life* belongs to this group of colorfully—if incongruously—upbeat images. Unlike his imitators, who were often engaged with ambitious chromatic theories, Picasso seems to have drawn his colors from everyday sources such as the wallpapers he clipped for his *papiers collés* and the spectrum of enamel house paints. Still, the example of Henri Matisse—and especially of boldly color-saturated works likes Matisse's *Red Studio* of 1911—doubtless played a role; and the lively, confetti-like dotting that appears prominently here seems to stem from a new, somewhat ironic and playful interest in the pointillist technique of the neo-Impressionist master Georges Seurat. In the spirit of the word fragment JOU—a segment of LE JOURNAL, the banner of a Paris newspaper, but also the root of the French verb *jouer*, meaning "to play"—the picture is replete with visual gamesmanship. The frame-within-a-frame at upper left (ambiguously denoting either a mirror or a picture on the wall) echoes the lower table molding that "frames" the still life, and the nail and string set atop the pearlike shape next to the cluster of grapes confounds the supposed horizontality of the tabletop, by suggesting that this passage depicts a hanging picture of a pear rather than the fruit itself. Witty, brilliant in hue, and light in spirit, the picture radiates a jaunty confidence, just on the eve of a grim period that would transform Europe into a theater of war, bring Eva's death, and break apart Picasso's artistic world.   K.V.

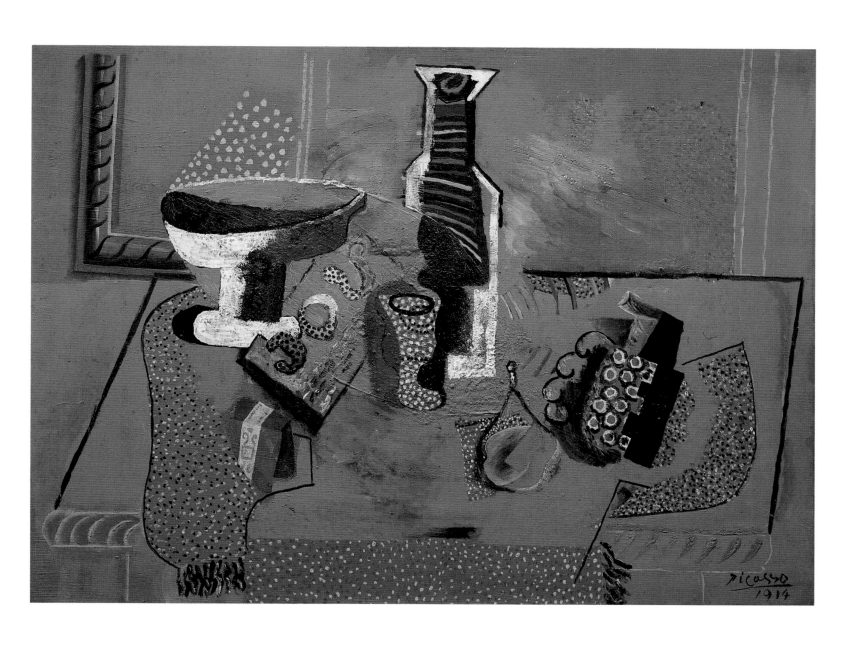

GREEN STILL LIFE. Avignon, summer 1914

Oil on canvas, 23½ × 31¼" (59.7 × 79.4 cm)
*Zervos II**, 485. D.R. 778. Lillie P. Bliss Collection*

Glass of Absinthe. *Paris, spring 1914*

In the midst of making constructions that exploded solid objects such as guitars into arrangements of planes (see Maquette for *Guitar*, p. 65), Picasso exceptionally decided to deal with a transparent object—the conical glass that cafés used to serve the potent liqueur absinthe—in terms of modeled forms. His doing so may seem a regression toward his first experiment with rendering fractured Cubist volumes in modeled matter (the *Woman's Head [Fernande]* of 1909; plate, p. 55), but by remaking the glass freestanding in its actual scale, and by including a real, appropriated object—the long-handled strainer that holds the sugar cube at the lip of the carafe—he commingled levels of reality in a way that prefigured the disturbing objects made by the Surrealists a decade or more later. The sculpture was originally modeled in wax, and from this wax form (destroyed in the casting process) six bronzes were made. Picasso painted each cast differently, but he often used, as here, a broadly handled pointillism that recalls his paintings of the time (see previous page); it may denote, in cartoonishly crude fashion, "atmosphere" or transparency. Similarly, in the Museum's version, large slashes of black seem to offer grossly reductive formulae for shading. Many writers have seen the flat or twisting planes within the opened-up volume of the glass as the elements of a distorted face, with the supporting cone as a neck and the strainer with its cube as a hat; it is doubtful Picasso intended that effect. More convincing is Brooks Adams's observation that Picasso's choice of theme was a charged and meaningful one. Around 1914, in the context of a debate that led to its being banned, absinthe was being widely denounced in France for its reputed corruption of the health and morals of society. Picasso's memorializing of this liquid may have represented, as Adams has argued, a contrary homage to the inspiring pleasures of disrupting one's senses, and to the intoxicating or dangerous freedoms of bohemian café life. K.V.

GLASS OF ABSINTHE. Paris, spring 1914
Painted bronze with absinthe spoon, 8½ × 6½ × 3⅜"
(21.6 × 16.4 × 8.5 cm); diameter at base, 2½" (6.4 cm)
Spies 36D. Gift of Mrs. Bertram Smith

Two Dancers. *Summer 1919*

In 1917, the poet Jean Cocteau pulled off the surprising feat of persuading Picasso to travel to Rome, in order to work with Serge Diaghilev's Ballets Russes in the preparation of a radically new ballet, *Parade*. Picasso disliked travel, and the voyage to Rome—especially in connection with a ballet troupe—suggested a return to the kinds of venerated traditions Cubism had overthrown. But then, many artists were already dismayed or confounded by the evidence, mounting since 1916, that Picasso had apparently turned his back on Cubism, in adopting a style of representational line drawing that recalled the mannered classicism of the nineteenth-century painter J.-A.-D. Ingres. The beau monde of the ballet—in contrast to the marginal world of circus and cabaret performers the artist had favored in his youthful bohemian days—might have seemed an all-too-ideal subject for this *retardataire,* self-consciously elegant manner. On closer inspection, though, *Two Dancers*, like other classicizing drawings done by Picasso at this time, also bears pungent inflections of his talents as a caricaturist, which act to subvert the idealizing blandness to which neoclassicism is often prey. The performers here seem, in fact, as much ridiculed as they are idealized. With tiny heads joined by goiterous necks to their rather stocky, pneumatic bodies, they gesture with a pretension to delicacy that is thoroughly belied by their sausagelike fingers; and the evident will to beauty in their uplifted gazes seems subtly mocked as a simpering pose. Picasso's marriage to one of Diaghilev's dancers, Olga Khokhlova, would soon pull his life further into the orbit of high society and bourgeois respectability, but an undercurrent of this malice toward upper-class artifices would never be absent from his work. It would eventually erupt, along with the latent grotesquery of these bodily distortions, in his surrealist imagery of the 1920s. Later, his re-embrace of classicism would be seen as part of what Cocteau called the *rappel a l'ordre*—a return to venerable disciplines in the arts as part of France's spiritual regeneration after the chaotic ravages of World War I—although Picasso's initiation of the style likely was not motivated by that ethos. K.V.

TWO DANCERS. Summer 1919
Pencil on paper, 12¼ × 9½" (31.0 × 23.9 cm)
Zervos XXIX, 430. P.P. 19.211
The John S. Newberry Collection

Three Musicians. *Fontainebleau, summer 1921*

In 1921, Picasso summered in the château town of Fontainebleau near Paris. Painting in a rented garage, he dedicated himself to several large canvases, including two versions of this composition (the other is now in the Philadelphia Museum of Art). They were the most imposing works Picasso had conceived in the style of Synthetic Cubism—a style that, in the aftermath of World War I, had come to seem rather outmoded. It was instead the neoclassicism the artist had initiated in the later 1910s (and used in alternating parallel with Synthetic Cubist stylizations) that was being increasingly celebrated, for its timely revivification of noble French and Mediterranean traditions. Indeed, many writers have seen *Three Musicians* as a summation of, and grand farewell to, a passing epoch in Picasso's art. But there may be other reasons, too, for the monumental somberness conveyed by the painting's dominantly dark palette and spectral light, and by the uncommonly grave, iconic address of this three-man band. Noting that the mingling of commedia dell'arte figures with a religious personage evokes a masked ball or carnival occasion, Theodore Reff has argued that Picasso here situated his own favorite avatar, the harlequin, as the guitar player between two poets who were comrades of his youth: on the left, a bulky Pierrot would represent Guillaume Apollinaire, who had died in 1917, and on the right, a more diminutive masked man in monk's garb would evoke Max Jacob, whose close friendship with Picasso had crumbled years before, and who had in fact entered a Benedictine monastery in the spring of 1921. The Philadelphia version of this nostalgic "reunion," or wake for the artist's bohemian youth, is more brightly upbeat. Here, with a more austere interlocking of broad, zigzagging planes and piquant details (such as the tiny hands), and with the addition of a dark dog beneath, the trio seems to play its jazzlike harmonies in a more muted key. The whimsical freedoms and decorative jauntiness of earlier Synthetic Cubist works persist, but the total air is of one of haunting solemnity. K.V.

THREE MUSICIANS. Fontainebleau,
summer 1921

Oil on canvas, 6'7" × 7'3¾" (200.7 × 222.9 cm)
Zervos IV, 331. P.P. 21.259
Mrs. Simon Guggenheim Fund

Nude Seated on a Rock. *Fontainebleau, summer 1921*

After honeymooning in Biarritz in 1918, Picasso and Olga Khokhlova spent almost every summer from 1919 through 1927 on the Riviera. The worlds of the ballet and the seashore merged in Picasso's imagination, inspiring countless pictures of nude bathers gamboling on halcyon beaches. Linear and elongated at first, Picasso's bathers begin around 1920 to swell into pneumatic, monumental figures. The change may have been impelled by Olga's pregnancy and by the birth, in February 1921, of their son Paolo. As in the *Two Nudes* of 1906 (plate, p. 45), the plump limbs and oversized heads and torsos of Picasso's bathers recall the physiques of small children. Parenthood may also have awakened Picasso's own childhood recollection of crawling under the dinner table "to look in awe" at the swollen legs of one of his aunts. As a child, he told Françoise Gilot, he often dreamed of legs and arms growing and shrinking to unnatural extremes. Whatever their personal motivation, Picasso's monumental bathers look back toward a long tradition of mannerist nudes extending from Michelangelo through Jean Goujon down to J.-A.-D. Ingres and Paul Cézanne. Recent scholars have stressed Picasso's interest in Pierre Auguste Renoir's late nudes, one of which Picasso purchased from his new dealer, Paul Rosenberg. There is an even more striking resemblance between Picasso's bathers and the sculptures of Aristide Maillol, whose massive figures were intended to evoke the image of a timeless Mediterranean culture. Despite its tiny dimensions and the delicate harmony of reds and blues, *Nude Seated on a Rock* gives the same impression of monumentality as the larger-than-life canvases that Picasso devoted to similar figures. This very monumentality tends to conceal the unnatural quality of the nude, constructed from balloonlike segments without any sign of bones or joints. In its own way, it is as abstract as the flattened figures of the contemporary *Three Musicians* (previous page). P.K.

NUDE SEATED ON A ROCK. Fontainebleau, summer 1921
Oil on wood, 6¼ × 4⅜" (15.8 × 11.1 cm)
Zervos IV, 309. P.P. 21. 254
James Thrall Soby Bequest

Studio with Plaster Head. *Juan-les-Pins, summer 1925*

Picasso painted this vivid still life in the Riviera town of Juan-les-Pins in the summer of 1925, at a time when his marriage to Olga Khokhlova was showing signs of severe strain. After the relative serenity of the neoclassical works initiated in the late 1910s, this was also a period when his art had begun to explore disquieting imagery, which would become steadily more attuned to (and admired by) the adherents of Surrealism. Many of the elements of classicism are still here, in the fragments of sculpture and the Italianate architecture of the background; and the rule of reason seems insisted upon by the right-angle drafting tool, the laurel branch, and the open book. One might in fact see the composition as presenting the attributes of the creative process—measure, research, and antique models—in a traditional allegory of art. Yet the portrait bust abandons noble decorum and evokes, in curly-haired caricature, the more trenchant realism of the late, troubled years of ancient Rome. Its aggressive black shadow, with what seems a comically large ear, actually yields a doorknoblike shape that Lydia Gassman has persuasively shown to be a (sometimes explicitly phallic) talismanic device Picasso frequently used to assert his own covert, controlling presence within numerous scenes of the 1920s and 1930s. The severed limbs, insistently hollow, evoke dismemberment, and the arm grasping a rod seems particularly premonitory of a key motif of pathetic suffering—the outstretched forearm of the downed soldier—in the *Guernica* mural (now in the Reina Sofía Art Center, Madrid) a dozen years later. The bust and body parts connect to a long series of still lifes Picasso had been working on through the previous spring. Here, they and other objects appear life-size in relation to the fleur-de-lis wallpaper (which also appears in the Tate Gallery's darkly dionysiac *Three Dancers*, painted earlier that summer), but colossal beside the miniaturized buildings and "sky," which are actually a small puppet theater, recalling earlier set designs for the ballet *Pulcinella*, that Picasso had made for his four-year-old son Paolo. K.V.

STUDIO WITH PLASTER HEAD. Juan-les-Pins,
summer 1925

Oil on canvas, 38⅝ × 51⅝" (97.9 × 131.1 cm)
Zervos V, 445. P.P. 25.086. Purchase

Seated Woman. *Paris, 1927*

As a child, Picasso had learned the trick of drawing figures and animals with a continuous line looping back on itself, so his hand never left the paper. In 1907 and in 1918, he used similar loops and scribbles for drawings of farmyard animals and reveling harlequins. Then, in 1924, his designs for the Léonide Massine ballet *Mercure* enlarged these "childish" scribbles to monumental scale, setting the stage for a new style of curvilinear Cubism. In works like *The Milliner's Workshop* of January 1926 (Musée National d'Art Moderne, Centre Georges Pompidou, Paris), interlacing curves divided figures and objects into independent shapes while uniting them within a continuous web; the complex design was clarified by the simple palette of black, white, and gray. The organic curves of this new work brought Picasso close to the pictorial vocabulary of Surrealists like Joan Miró, André Masson, and Jean Arp. The *Seated Woman* of 1927 represents the culmination of a long series of heads and figures deriving from *The Milliner's Workshop*. Here, the curvilinear web is limited to the figure itself, silhouetted against the corner of a room. Several different heads seem to overlap, with the woman's profile emerging from their intersection. The curving strips of her pink and white arms encircle her red and gray torso, divided by a schematic shadow descending in a dark band from the back of her head. Despite the subtle play of earthy colors, the composition remains fundamentally tonal, organized around steplike divisions among dark, light, and intermediate areas. Scholars long regarded the "biomorphic" shapes of Picasso's 1926–27 paintings as a product of purely formal experimentation. Recently, however, it has been discovered that Picasso's relationship with Marie-Thérèse Walter, the muse of 1930s masterpieces like *Girl Before a Mirror* (plate, p. 101), actually began in the mid-1920s. Picasso's new formal vocabulary may thus reflect her presence. In other works related to *Seated Woman*, the overlapping heads clearly belong to embracing lovers; and the painting's "moon-face" profile later emerges as a recurrent symbol for Marie-Thérèse. On the other hand, the figure as a whole seems restrained—even matronly—in comparison to the vibrant sensuality of the later canvas. P.K.

SEATED WOMAN. Paris, 1927
Oil on wood, 51⅛ × 38¼" (129.9 × 96.8 cm)
Zervos VII, 77. P.P. 27.016
Gift of James Thrall Soby

Painter and Model Knitting. *Paris, late 1927*

Ambroise Vollard had given Picasso his first show in Paris, and Picasso continued for years to turn to him when he needed money in a hurry. By the late 1920s, Picasso had forged a solid relationship with Paul Rosenberg, a more stylish dealer with international connections. Nonetheless, he was willing when Vollard asked him to illustrate a deluxe edition of Honoré de Balzac's story *The Unknown Masterpiece.* Over the previous thirty years, Vollard had published a remarkable series of books with illustrations by Pierre Auguste Renoir, Auguste Rodin, Pierre Bonnard, Marc Chagall, and other artists. Furthermore, Picasso was intrigued by Balzac's story, the tale of an imaginary seventeenth-century painter who labors for a decade over his masterpiece, a nude, only to produce a virtual abstraction comprehensible only to himself. Much of the book was illustrated with woodcut versions of drawings that Picasso had done in summer 1924, transforming figures and still lifes into abstract "constellations" of dots and lines. (Compare p. 91). But Picasso also executed thirteen new etchings specifically for Vollard's volume. In this, the best-known of the series, the bearded, bohemian artist carefully scrutinizes his model, but what he draws on his canvas is a geometric whorl of curves and angles, much like Picasso's contemporary *Seated Woman* (previous page). Everyday reality is confronted with its translation into platonic forms. Underscoring the contrast between reality and ideal, the model is not one of the beautiful young women who typically appear in Picasso's prints (compare p. 103), but a homely, middle-aged housekeeper, intent on her knitting. The juxtaposition of model and canvas also provides a kind of object lesson in how to read Picasso's pictures. The viewer is invited to pick out the curves in the canvas corresponding to the recognizable contours of the model's face, hair, shoulders, and hips. Insisting on the conceptual character of modern art, the canvas also includes the outlines of the model's breast and belly, anatomical features that are not visible in the "real" figure. In 1938, Picasso would move into a studio on the rue des Grands-Augustins in Paris, where Balzac's story had taken place. P.K.

**PAINTER AND MODEL KNITTING, plate IV
from LE CHEF D'OEUVRE INCONNU by Honoré
de Balzac. Published Paris, Ambroise Vollard,
Editeur, 1931 (print executed Paris, late 1927)**
Etching, plate: 7 9/16 × 10 15/16" (19.3 × 27.8 cm)
Geiser/Baer I, 126. The Louis E. Stern Collection

Guitars. *Juan-les-Pins, 1924*

Gertrude Stein noted the importance of the "calligraphic tendency" in Picasso's work of the 1910s and 1920s, providing a middle way between the extremes of realism and abstraction. This tendency, she wrote, had its "most intense moment" in Picasso's décor for the 1924 ballet *Mercure*: it was "written, so simply written, no painting, pure calligraphy." Picasso's spring 1924 designs for *Mercure* posed linear, curving figures against a backdrop decorated with diagrammatic stars. As his drawings progressed, the stars migrated to the interiors of the figures, evolving into the dots marking the junctures of breasts, knees and feet. The following summer, at Juan-les-Pins, Picasso filled twenty-five pages of a notebook with drawings of guitars, still lifes, and figures reduced to virtually abstract arrangements of parallel lines and curves, punctuated by dots at their crossings and termini. Here, line functions simultaneously as contour and texture. The near-abstraction of the 1924 sketches inspired Picasso to have them reproduced as wood engravings and included with the illustrations for *The Unknown Masterpiece*, devoted to the theme of the artistic tension between representation and "pure" creation (see previous page). Alfred Barr's well-known description of these designs as "constellations" of dots and lines suggests their affinity with the 1940–41 "Constellations" of Joan Miró, an extraordinary series of colored drawings whose evenly-spaced, rhythmic patterns anticipate the "allover" compositions of Jackson Pollock and the Abstract Expressionists. Indeed, there is an echo of Picasso's designs in Pollock's curves of poured paint, punctuated by swells and spatters. P.K.

GUITARS, sheet N from LE CHEF-D'OEUVRE INCONNU by Honoré de Balzac. Published Paris, Ambroise Vollard, Editeur, 1931 (reproduced drawings executed Juan-les-Pins, 1924)
Wood engraving of dot and line drawing, page: 12 15/16 × 9 15/16" (33.0 × 25.2 cm)
The Louis E. Stern Collection

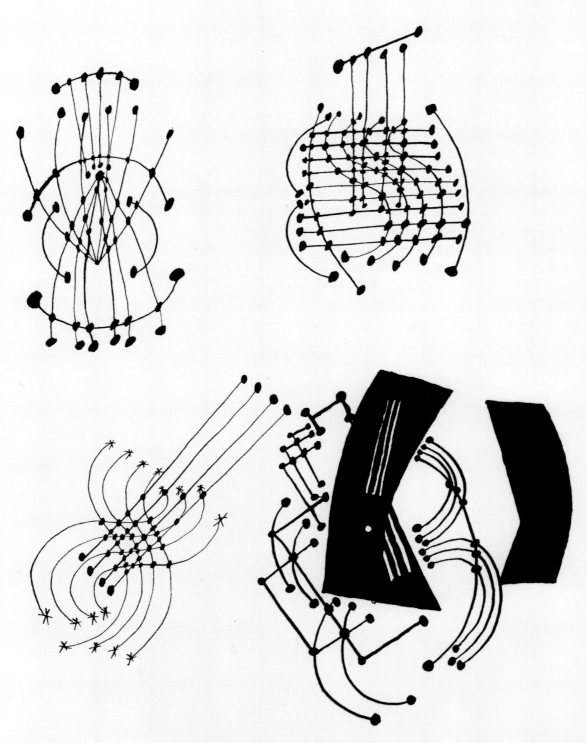

The Studio. *Paris, 1928*

Picasso began thinking about the motif of painter and model in late 1925 or early 1926—around the same time that he met Marie-Thérèse Walter. In a notebook from this period, studies of Marie-Thérèse alternate with sketches of Olga Picasso teaching the five-year-old Paolo how to ride a bicycle. One sketch shows the lesson taking place in Picasso's studio; this composition was enlarged into a mural-scale canvas, preserving the pose of the artist hunched over his palette, but replacing the mother and child with a recumbent nude. Picasso reworked the same composition in a large 1927 canvas titled *Painter and Model,* and revised it yet again in *The Studio,* substituting a plaster bust for the living model. The 1926 version of this composition was apparently painted as a pendant to *The Milliner's Workshop* (see commentary, p. 86), with figures linked by a similar web of interlaced curves. In subsequent versions, Picasso gradually suppressed the curves in favor of a spartan vocabulary of straight lines and angles. The background of *The Studio* is divided into a series of rectangles. In the foreground, the painter, the table, the fruit bowl, and the plaster bust are represented by polygons and ovoids suggesting three dimensions while remaining flat. Despite its near-abstraction, *The Studio* seems haunted by the ghost of the nude Marie-Thérèse. Although the painter is studying a horizontal still-life arrangement of fruit bowl and bust, he is standing before a narrow vertical canvas clearly meant for a figure. The almond shapes representing eyes and mouth had served, in the 1927 *Painter and Model,* to draw an explicit equation between these apertures and the female sex. The reiterated eye-vagina of the painter's face now seems to insist that visual impregnation is a necessary prelude to artistic creation. As Picasso told Geneviève Laporte, years later: "Every artist is a woman." P.K.

THE STUDIO. Paris, winter 1927–28;
dated 1928

Oil on canvas, 59" × 7'7" (149.9 × 231.2 cm)
Zervos VII, 142. P.P. 27.075
Gift of Walter P. Chrysler, Jr.

Project for a Monument to Guillaume Apollinaire. *1928*

Picasso's friend Guillaume Apollinaire died in November 1918, succumbing to influenza while Paris celebrated the end of World War I. Three years later, his admirers formed a committee to construct a monument for his grave in the cemetery of Père Lachaise. For the design, they naturally turned to Picasso. His first proposals, submitted in late 1927, depicted swollen, sexualized bathers. The literary members of the committee were horrified: they wanted to commemorate Apollinaire the poet and war hero, not Apollinaire the pornographer. Picasso then proposed a series of abstract figures constructed from wires or bars. There were numerous precedents for these in his earlier work. He had originally intended to construct his fall 1909 sculpture of a woman's head (plate, p. 55) from open, interlacing strands. His designs for the June 1924 ballet *Mercure* included several figures made from long rattan strips, and wirelike figures and constructions frequently appear in his 1924–28 sketchbooks. But, as Alan Bowness has noted, it was not until 1928 that Jacques Lipchitz's exhibition of welded iron sculptures revealed a way for Picasso to realize his designs in permanent form. Working with Julio Gonzalez, an accomplished sculptor and metalworker, Picasso welded together iron rods and sheet metal to make models of his designs for the Apollinaire monument. Despite their family resemblance to the simplified linear figures of the 1927–28 *Studio* (previous page), these designs were from the outset complex and three-dimensional. Picasso began with abstract combinations of interpenetrating cones and pyramids, and then modified them to form structures recalling the human body. Here, the figure's torso is represented three times: as a triangular pyramid, as a suspended circle, and as a cantilevered rectangle. The arms are elongated pyramids stretching forward from the circle; at their termini, long, curving rods suggest the grasping motion of hands. Picasso's idea of "drawing in space," and his subsequent incorporation of found objects, had a revolutionary effect on modern art, influencing contemporaries like Gonzalez, younger sculptors like Alexander Calder and David Smith, and later artists like Richard Stankiewicz and Anthony Caro. The Apollinaire committee, however, rejected his welded sculptures just as they had his earlier proposals. P.K.

PROJECT FOR A MONUMENT TO GUILLAUME APOLLINAIRE (Intermediate Model). 1962; enlarged version, after 1928 original maquette
Painted steel, 6'6" × 62⅞" × 29½" (198 × 159.4 × 72.3 cm), including base. Spies 68B. Gift of the artist

Bather and Cabin. *Dinard, August 1928*

During the summers of 1927 and 1928, Picasso vacationed with Olga and Paolo at chic retreats of Europe's well-to-do: first Cannes, on the Riviera, then, in 1928, the Brittany coast resort of Dinard. Within the high-society holidays, however, maelstroms of resentment and deception roiled. At odds with Olga and chafed by their bourgeois lifestyle, Picasso had—apparently as early as 1926—picked up the teenaged Marie-Thérèse Walter on the streets of Paris and made her his secret mistress. At Dinard he hid her, conveniently for assignations, in a nearby hostel for little girls. These tensions of the time helped fuel an aggressive new burst of figural imagery, often set in bathing scenes on the beach. At Cannes, apparently with the ambition of erecting colossal figures along the seaside drive, Picasso's drawings and paintings deformed or disassembled human anatomy in impossible but realistically volumetric, specifically sculptural terms. Transforming roaring-twenties bathers into elephantine monsters or dolmens, he drew on deep wells of personal memory (such as a childhood fascination with an under-the-table view of his aunts' huge legs) but also on the biomorphic personages and stones-and-bones phantasms recently invented by Surrealists such as Joan Miró and Yves Tanguy. Picasso's disgust with Olga, and his lust for Marie-Thérèse, almost certainly informed the resultant "bathers;" but as usual in Picasso, animus and eros, like the identities of people, and the poles of sexuality, are not susceptible to easy separation. This little scene, with its stick-and-boomerang female anatomy and a lurking male shadow behind, contains two elements that haunted the Cannes and Dinard beach scenes: the cabana and the key. Lydia Gassman has convincingly shown that Picasso took the omnipresent cabana not from the beaches he was on—where they were rare and out of fashion—but from the Spanish coast of his childhood. Fused in memory with the similar shapes of cemetery crypts, it had, Gassman argues, a malleable symbolism involving Picasso's sense of the dark, protected interiority of his unconscious. It is frequently paired with a female creature who tries, as here, to open it with a key—a sexually suggestive metaphor, and an object for which the Surrealists in general, and Picasso personally, had an abiding fascination.   K.V.

BATHER AND CABIN. Dinard, August 1928
Oil on canvas, painted area: 8½ × 6¼" (21.5 × 15.8 cm). Zervos VII, 211. P.P. 28.171
Hillman Periodicals Fund

Face of Marie-Thérèse. *Paris, fall 1928*

In fall 1928, when he executed this lithograph as the frontispiece for the deluxe edition of André Salmon's *Picasso*, the artist had just turned forty-seven. His subject, Marie-Thérèse Walter, was now nineteen. The disparity between their ages was no longer quite as scandalous as it might have seemed a few years earlier. Still, as Robert Rosenblum has remarked, "we may be astonished by the master's temerity in half-revealing his personal secret within the public context of his art." Alfred Barr noted the "'close-up' cutting" of Picasso's shadowy portrait. In movies, close-ups usually reveal a character's private feelings. But Marie-Thérèse here remains as distant and unknowable as a classical goddess. The tight framing of the image seems to express Picasso's desire to confine his mistress in solitude, away from the eyes of the world, at the same time that he boasts of her beauty. Eliminating the mass of the surrounding head, Picasso flattens the face into a stylized mask. At the same time, his chiaroscuro shading intensifies the sculptural quality of the facial features, so that the image seems less like a print than a photograph of a bas-relief. Indeed, when Picasso returned to carved and modeled sculpture (after his experiments with welded construction; see p. 94), he executed a large plaster relief of Marie-Thérèse's head, seen from the same angle as in this print. P.K.

FACE OF MARIE-THÉRÈSE (VISAGE DE MARIE-THÉRÈSE). Paris, fall 1928
Lithograph, comp.: 8⅛ × 5 9/16" (20.6 × 14.1 cm)
Geiser/Baer I, 243. Mourlot 23
Gift of Abby Aldrich Rockefeller

58/75

Girl Before a Mirror. *Boisgeloup, March 1932*

Picasso may actually have been involved with Marie-Thérèse Walter for five years before her curvaceous blond beauty erupted recognizably in the sculptures and paintings of 1931 that scholars previously saw as marking the first bloom of the affair. These are among the most erotically ripe images Picasso ever produced, and their centerpiece is this exceptional remaking of a traditional theme. A woman looking into a mirror had long been a vehicle for exposing the fallacies of vanity and the fragility of beauty—most explicitly, by having the mirror show the body in decrepitude or death. Picasso's motif is instead a fervent homage to the fecund power of sexuality. A marriage at the highest level of his gifts as an inventor of form and as a colorist, the picture is at once primal and subtle, with a magic sense of presence that seems—as per the echoes of stained glass in the brilliant hues and black outlines—almost sacramental. The circular head on the left divides into a white-haloed, lilac-tender profile of innocence, and a searingly hot, rouged and gilded far side. This sun-and-moon, virgin-and-whore duality is then given back in the mirror by an even more lunar head with nocturnal eyes, conjuring some still-deeper subconscious state. The bodies below swell with the forms of seeds, fruits, and sprouts in visual metaphors of female fertility. Yet the male presence is implied here, too, in the testicular breasts and erect outstretched arm that suggest physical as well as psychic intercourse. Picasso's swelling modeled sculptures of this period similarly fuse male and female references, in busts built from genital forms, as if to suggest the merger of desire and its object, and the loss of boundaries in the union of erotic pleasures. He may also imply his pervasive presence here through the patterned wallpaper that recalls the costume of his avatar, the harlequin. Picasso declared this his favorite among the harvest of paintings he produced in the spring of 1932—a group whose luxuriance and particularly vivid coloring may reflect the artist's competitive response to a brilliant Matisse exhibition mounted in Paris the previous summer. K.V.

GIRL BEFORE A MIRROR. Boisgeloup, March 1932
Oil on canvas, 64 × 51¼" (162.3 × 130.2 cm)
Zervos VII, 379. P.P. 32.033
Gift of Mrs. Simon Guggenheim

Model and Sculptor with His Sculpture. *March 17, 1933.*

From the Vollard Suite. *Published Paris, 1939*

After his revolutionary experiments with welding (see p. 95), Picasso returned in 1931–32 to more conventional methods of sculpturemaking. Working in the stables of the château he had purchased at Boisgeloup as a refuge for himself and Marie-Thérèse Walter, he whittled tall, narrow figures from sticks of wood, and modeled larger-than-life heads from great balls of plaster. These were followed, in spring 1933, by a suite of forty-six etchings dedicated to the theme of "The Sculptor's Studio," later integrated into the larger sequence known as the *Vollard Suite* (see pp. 104–07). Here, as Roland Penrose noted: "Picasso transposed the scene from twentieth-century Normandy to the mythical atmosphere of ancient Greece. The sculptor became a bearded Athenian, nude like the heroes and crowned with garlands. With him is his muse, sometimes posing for him but more often resting on a couch beside him, naked and beautiful, in contemplation of the work she has inspired." Critics have often stressed the disparity, in these prints, between the naturalistic image of the model and the abstract or surreal appearance of the sculpted heads inspired by her. (Compare *Painter and Model Knitting,* p. 89.) But the sculptures reproduced in these prints can be seen equally well as symbols of shared experience. As John Berger argues, Picasso's goal was not to represent Marie-Thérèse, but to evoke the pleasure of their lovemaking—to trace what William Blake called the "lineaments of satisfied desire." Typically, tubular nose and rounded brow combine into an image of the male sex, while a vaginal mouth is nestled between swollen cheeks like buttocks or thighs. What sculptor and model contemplate, in the prints, is not an abstraction but the image of their mutual bliss. P.K.

MODEL AND SCULPTOR WITH HIS SCULPTURE (MODÈLE ET SCULPTEUR AVEC SA SCULPTURE). March 17, 1933. From the *Vollard Suite.* Published Paris, Ambroise Vollard Éditeur, 1939 (plates executed 1930–37)
Etching, plate: 10½ × 7⁹⁄₁₆" (26.7 × 19.3 cm)
Geiser/Baer II, 300. Abby Aldrich Rockefeller Fund

Bacchanal with Minotaur. *May 18, 1933*

Blind Minotaur Guided Through a Starry Night by Marie-Thérèse with a Pigeon. *December 3, 1934–January 1, 1935*

Faun Unveiling a Sleeping Girl. *June 12, 1936*

From the Vollard Suite. *Published Paris, 1939*

In 1933, Picasso came into contact with the master printer Roger Lacourière, and through his studio became intrigued anew with etching, especially the broader tonal possibilities of a sugar-lift aquatint technique Lacourière commanded. The rich, raking afternoon light in *Faun Unveiling a Sleeping Girl* (opposite), and the velvety nocturne of *Blind Minotaur Guided Through a Starry Night* (plate, p. 107) exemplify that aquatint process. The rediscovery of the medium seemed to prompt Picasso to extend his earlier neoclassical imagery into the creation of a dominantly idyllic Mediterranean world, bound together by the fragments of a narrative thread, in a series of one hundred etchings that would be published together in 1939 by the dealer Ambroise Vollard. While many of the scenes in the *Vollard Suite* involve mature, hirsute sculptors in idyllic repose with their lissome blond models (see p. 106)—an idealization of the artist's twice-her-age relationship with Marie-Thérèse—some of the prime recurring protagonists are part-human, part-animal: the faun in *Faun Unveiling a Sleeping Girl*, for example, but especially the bull-headed beast of *Blind Minotaur* and *Bacchanal with Minotaur* (plate, p. 106). Picasso's image of himself as part-animal dates back to early self-caricature, but hybrid "monsters" became more prominent in his imagery of the 1930s, when the displacement of reason by animal instinct connected directly to the ideals of the Surrealists. Of the relatively gentle hooved-and-horned faun who steals in to unveil a dozing beauty with delicate reserve (in revivification of the "sleepwatcher" theme of *Meditation*; plate, p. 33) Picasso later said that the beast was pondering whether the dreaming woman might love him *because* he was a monster. The minotaur is treated on the other hand as a less reflective, burlier captive of impulse and of fate. In Greek legend he was a savage, man-eating terror that lived in a labyrinth on Crete. But Picasso's could be by turns a hearty companion in Bacchanalian revels, then a violent beast possessed by rapine lust, and finally a tragic victim, punished by blinding or death. Picasso's immediate travails with Olga may have figured in the implied self-pity of these latter scenes—where Marie-Thérèse is less love object and more often a childlike, sympathetic witness—but the cycle of the Minotaur's destiny also owes to this Spaniard's lifelong fascination with the bullfight, and its conjunction of animal power with ritual sacrifice. K.V.

**FAUN UNVEILING A SLEEPING GIRL (JUPITER
AND ANTIOPE, AFTER REMBRANDT) (FAUNE
DÉVOILANT UNE DORMEUSE (JUPITER ET
ANTIOPE, D'APRÈS REMBRANDT), state VI.
June 12, 1936. From the *Vollard Suite*. Pub-
lished Paris, Ambroise Vollard Éditeur, 1939
(plates executed 1930–37)**

Aquatint, lift-ground aquatint, and engraving,
plate: 12 7/16 × 16 7/16" (31.6 × 41.7 cm)
Geiser/Baer III, 609
Abby Aldrich Rockefeller Fund

**BACCHANAL WITH MINOTAUR (SCÈNE
BACHIQUE AU MINOTAURE), state III. May 18,
1933. From the *Vollard Suite*. Published Paris,
Ambroise Vollard Éditeur, 1939 (plates executed 1930–37)**

Etching, plate: 11¹¹⁄₁₆ × 14³⁄₈" (29.7 × 36.6 cm)
Geiser/Baer II, 351. Abby Aldrich Rockefeller Fund

**BLIND MINOTAUR GUIDED THROUGH A
STARRY NIGHT BY MARIE-THÉRÈSE WITH A
PIGEON (MINOTAURE AVEUGLE GUIDÉ PAR
MARIE-THÉRÈSE AU PIGEON DANS UNE NUIT
ÉTOILÉE), state IV. Between December 3, 1934
and January 1, 1935. From the *Vollard Suite*.
Published Paris, Ambroise Vollard Éditeur,
1939 (plates executed 1930–37)**

*Aquatint, drypoint, and engraving, plate: 9 ¾ ×
13 ⁹⁄₁₆" (24.7 × 34.5 cm). Geiser/Baer II, 437*
Abby Aldrich Rockefeller Fund

Minotauromachy. *Paris, March 23, 1935*

Nineteen thirty-five was a year of dramatic changes in Picasso's life. In June, provoked by the discovery that her husband's young mistress was pregnant, Olga finally left him. Her departure seems to have thrown him into deep depression, unable to paint for months on end. The birth of his daughter Maya, in September, represented the culmination of his long passion for Marie-Thérèse Walter; but it also signified unmistakably that she was no longer the child-woman who had first attracted him. It is not clear whether these impending crises had come to a head in late March, when Picasso executed the plate of the *Minotauromachy*. But the picture's complex symbolism seems to sum up his troubled and contradictory feelings about women, love, and sex. At center, the female picador with bared breasts, slumped over the back of a wounded horse, derives from a series of bullfight drawings dating back as far as 1919. Beginning with the image of a mounted picador trying to weaken a bull, the series comes to focus on the vengeful bull goring his tormentor's horse—a metaphor, in Picasso's eyes, for the passionate struggle of sex. Reason overthrown by passion is incarnated in the figure of the unconscious picador, while the equation of wound and vagina evokes an aura of sexual violence. Originally associated with Olga, the drama of bull and horse becomes identified, by the mid-1930s, with Marie-Thérèse. The other characters of the *Minotauromachy* assume their roles in relation to the central image of sexual trauma. At left, the bearded sculptor, a frequent stand-in for Picasso (see, for example, p. 103), climbs a ladder toward a romantic rendezvous. At right, he reappears in the guise of an Oedipus-Minotaur punished by blindness for his sexual transgressions. (Compare previous page.) The child-woman with flowers and a candle, offering guidance and forgiveness, seems like another avatar of Marie-Thérèse, as do the spectators at the window above. A year later, in the canvas of *Guernica* (fig. 4, p. 17), many of these motifs would be reworked as images of public rather than private trauma.   P.K.

4/50   Picasso

MINOTAUROMACHY (LA MINOTAURO-
MACHIE), state VII. Paris, March 23, 1935
Etching and engraving, plate: 19 ½ × 27 ⅜"
(49.6 × 69.6 cm). Geiser/Baer III, 573
Abby Aldrich Rockefeller Fund

Dream and Lie of Franco. *Paris, 1937*

Picasso's personal life had been in turmoil in 1936, given the bitter machinations of his legal separation from Olga, and for a while he stopped painting. When he resumed work, he found his personal woes conflated with the larger agonies of an approaching world war. Still strongly tied to Spain despite his many years in France, he was a fervent partisan of the Republican cause in the Spanish Civil War, which broke out in July 1936, and an equally ferocious opponent of the fascist forces led by General Franco. His most important statement on this conflict was, of course, the large mural *Guernica* (fig. 4, p. 17), completed in the summer of 1937 as a response to the bombing of a Basque village by Franco's German allies, and as a centerpiece of the Spanish pavilion at the 1937 International Exposition in Paris. But Picasso had already launched a visual attack against Franco in these two composites of postcard-size etchings that may originally have been intended for sale individually, to raise funds for the Republicans. In the second sheet of images, the upturned heads of shrieking women and the echoes of traditional Christian scenes of The Massacre of the Innocents connect directly to *Guernica* (the bottom three panels and the woman's head in the second tier were in fact added to the plate in June, after work on the mural had begun). More particular to this occasion, though, is the grotesque figure who runs rampant in the first sheet, and is confronted by the noble bull in the second. The artist described him in an accompanying free-verse, stream-of-consciousness poem as "an evil-omened polyp . . . placed upon the ice-cream cone of codfish fried in the scabs of his lead-ox heart . . . his mouth full of the clinch-bug jelly of his words." Often astride a steed (on one occasion a pig), this character seems a blackly absurd inversion of the Spanish chivalric ideal, a St. James or Don Quixote of evil. Drawing on folk cartoons as well as American comic strips (of which he was a fan), Picasso turned the format of humor to the task of rage, just as he used the knight to skewer knavery, and the distortions of eros to conjure the form of repulsion—drawings show that the polyp's tuberlike form emerged in parallel with a series of twisted, deforming variations on the head and breasts of Marie-Thérèse. As elsewhere in modern art, the form of the unprecedented or the unspeakable is found through the subversion of the familiar, and by twisting conventions of levity or beauty. Simple scatology plays a role as well: when asked what his hideous polyp-man resembled, Picasso later said simply *"etron"*—a turd. K.V.

DREAM AND LIE OF FRANCO I (SUEÑO Y MENTIRA DE FRANCO I). Published Paris, by the artist, 1937
Etching and lift-ground aquatint, plate: 12½ × 16⅝" (31.7 × 42.2 cm). Geiser/Baer III, 615
The Louis E. Stern Collection. 973.64.1

DREAM AND LIE OF FRANCO II (SUEÑO Y MENTIRA DE FRANCO II). Published Paris, by the artist, 1937
Etching and lift-ground aquatint, plate: 12½ × 16⅝" (31.7 × 42.2 cm). Geiser/Baer III, 616
The Louis E. Stern Collection

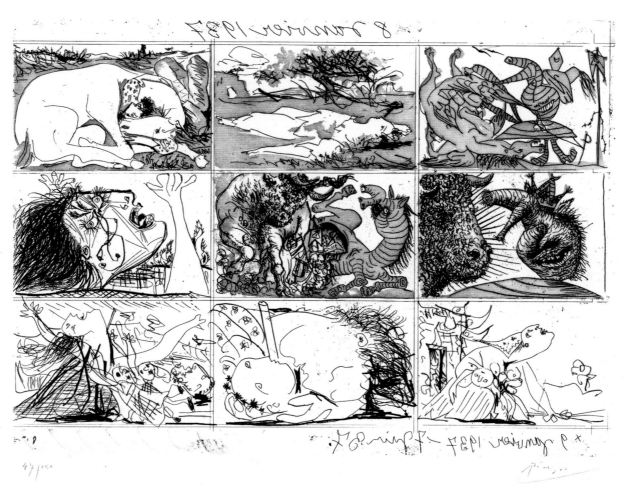

Maya in a Sailor Suit. *January 1938*

Born in September 1935, Marie-Thérèse Walter's daughter Maya was a little more than two years old when Picasso painted this portrait of her dressed in a sailor suit and holding a child's butterfly net. Picasso is sometimes said to have executed it in a deliberately childish manner, matching style to subject. Although this may be true of details like the sausage-shaped loops representing fingers, the overall composition has virtually nothing in common with a typical child's drawing. Where a child would outline the torso as a vertical oval with sticklike appendages, Picasso paints Maya's body as an arrangement of flat colored areas. The torso seems strangely truncated, vertically, while the legs are represented by widely spaced bands. In these respects, the composition recalls the Douanier Rousseau's portraits of children, often cited as an influence. The configuration of the head—seen simultaneously full-face and in profile—is pure Picasso, appearing in numerous contemporary images of both Marie-Thérèse and Dora Maar. A child would be unlikely to arrive at the simple yet allusive form of the figure-eight ear, a recurrent hieroglyph suggesting keyholes and infinity. Similarly, the crude palette of blue, green, and turquoise is enlivened by sophisticated accents of orange and violet. The inscription, "Picasso," on the headband of Maya's sailor's cap (compare the seal on the beret of the 1914 *Student with Pipe,* p. 73) led many early viewers to read this canvas as a self-portrait. Picasso willingly agreed, disingenuously telling one visitor that "he had painted himself as a sailor because he always wore a sailor's striped undershirt." As one scholar has suggested, by merging his image with his daughter's, Picasso may have hoped to appropriate some of her youth and vitality. P.K.

MAYA IN A SAILOR SUIT. January 1938
Oil on canvas, 47⅞ × 34" (121.6 × 86.3 cm)
Zervos IX, 104. Gift of Jacqueline Picasso in honor of the Museum's continuous commitment to Pablo Picasso's art

Night Fishing at Antibes. *Antibes, August 1939*

The summer of 1939 was one of evil portent on several levels in Picasso's life. His mother had recently passed away, and shortly after he left Paris for the Riviera, Ambroise Vollard (with whom he had just completed final arrangements for the publication of the *Vollard Suite* etchings; see pp. 102–07) also died. Moreover, the final defeat of the Republicans in Spain offered yet another signal that a broader war was at hand; by the end of the summer, France was mobilizing to fight Germany. Knowing this fraught context, writers have often searched this watery nocturne—the sole canvas that occupied Picasso during the end of July and first part of August—for deeper meanings. Although it has the scale of *Guernica* (and shares with it the pyramidal composition topped by a light source), Picasso painted it without any preparatory studies, on an unstretched canvas fixed to the wall of his rented apartment. Its immediate source lay in scenes he witnessed on evening strolls along the old port of Antibes, beneath the towers of the Château Grimaldi (now the Musée Picasso d'Antibes), which appear on the left. Fisherman are shown using acetylene lamps to lure and dazzle fish, while moths flap around the light and tourists observe from the quai. Dora Maar, who was with Picasso at the time, has identified the bicycling coquette, who salaciously darts a pointed tongue at the twin scoops of her ice-cream cone, as herself, and the other woman as Jacqueline Lamba, the wife of the chief Surrealist, André Breton. Yet despite this plausible quality of anecdotal reportage, it has been argued that models in older art helped shape the composition, that the combination of decorative, childlike distortions and nocturnal mystery owe something to Paul Klee, and that such charged sources as manuscripts of the apocalypse and the lamplit massacre of Francisco de Goya's *The Third of May, 1808* of 1814–15 may underlie the ostensibly ritualized, sacrificial slaying on which the scene centers. Detailed speculations about encoded meanings have been inconclusive, however, and the somewhat goofy, even slapdash charm of the pie-headed sailor, his drop-nose partner, the bug-eyed crab, and the other denizens of this comically eerie picture remains intriguingly out of step with its scale and its circumstances. K.V.

NIGHT FISHING AT ANTIBES. Antibes,
August 1939
Oil on canvas, 6'9" × 11'4" (205.8 × 345.4 cm)
Zervos IX, 316. Mrs. Simon Guggenheim Fund

Woman Dressing Her Hair. *Royan, June 1940*

Even after his separation from Olga and the birth of his daughter Maya, Picasso continued to conceal his relationship with Marie-Thérèse Walter. As if to re-create the tension that had previously existed between Olga and Marie-Thérèse, he began a new liaison with Dora Maar, a Surrealist photographer who had captured his attention at a café one evening by methodically stabbing the table around her hand. Drawn to Dora's anguish and intelligence, Picasso depicted her repeatedly as a weeping woman, a "suffering machine" on the border between animate and inanimate. After the outbreak of World War II, in September 1939, Picasso moved to Royan, a port on the Atlantic coast, lodging Dora in his hotel and Marie-Thérèse and Maya in a nearby villa. In May 1940, the Germans invaded France. Several dated studies for *Woman Dressing Her Hair* suggest that the picture was planned and painted in the interim before the Germans' arrival in Royan on June 23. But the claustrophobic setting—a bare room shrunk to the dimensions of a cardboard box—clearly anticipates the experience of life under occupation. Divided between glare and shadow, the figure seems to be caught in the beam of military searchlights. (Picasso had in fact borrowed several powerful spotlights from Dora's studio.) Picasso's starting point, as usual, was a formal idea: the inscription of the woman's breasts around an arrangement of pinwheeling curves, one rising, the other falling. Detail by detail, the woman represents a series of brilliant solutions to formal problems: she is seen simultaneously from front and side, near and far. But the overall effect is grotesque. As one indignant critic exclaimed: "Is this a woman or a trussed fowl?" Picasso's terrifying evocation of the body as carcass inspired a new wave of Surrealism among postwar painters like Francis Bacon. P.K.

WOMAN DRESSING HER HAIR (FEMME ASSISE).
Royan, June 1940
Oil on canvas, 51¼ × 38¼ (130.1 × 97.1 cm)
Zervos X, 302. Louise Reinhardt Smith Bequest

The Charnel House. *Paris, 1945*

Picasso chose not to flee France when the Germans invaded in 1940. He lived throughout the occupation in his studio building on the rue des Grands-Augustins, clandestinely in touch with friends in the Resistance, and generally exempted by the Germans from strict control. Signs of his precarious existence, and of the plight of a world at war, entered his work only obliquely, as in still lifes that centered on animal and human skulls, and in a general sobriety of tone. But after the liberation of Paris in 1944, he undertook this, his most pointed confrontation with current events since *Guernica* (fig. 4, p. 17). Reprises here of *Guernica*'s pyramidal organization, newsprint grisaille, and pathos formulae make *The Charnel House* seem in many senses a pendant coda, or elegiac, entwining decrescendo, to the spiky, explosive force of that earlier protest against war's onset. The slaughtered and jumbled family group—a hog-tied father, bleeding mother, and inert child, beneath a table with casserole and pitcher—may have originated, as Dora Maar claimed, in a scene of domestic murder Picasso saw in a Spanish film. The picture has long been associated, though, with the horrific piles of corpses discovered on the liberation of German concentration camps. While photographs of such scenes were scarcely seen at the time, recent research by Gertje Utley has shown how Picasso, in the evolution of the composition, absorbed news of the camps from the advancing allied front. She also reveals how he adjusted to a rapidly changing political climate in Paris, especially as regards the outlook of the Communist party, which he would officially join shortly before *The Charnel House* was first shown in the spring of 1945. Originally, the picture had overtones of redemption and hope, with the upraised fist suggestive, as in *Guernica,* of warrior defiance (and specifically of the Communist salute), and with a crowing rooster in the background, symbolic of a new dawn for France. But in parallel with the advent of a harsher, more recriminating ideology of vengeance that emerged in French society as the euphoria of liberation receded, Picasso modified these elements, to concentrate on the tangled mass of brutality's aftermath. Nonetheless, here as elsewhere, Picasso's use of abstracted forms and his elimination of specific, didactic references made his work a more universal human statement, at odds with the unambiguous "social realism" the party sought from its artist-adherents. K.V.

THE CHARNEL HOUSE. Paris, 1944–45;
dated 1945
Oil and charcoal on canvas, 6'6⅝" × 8'2½"
(199.8 × 250.1 cm). Zervos XIV, 76
Mrs. Sam A. Lewisohn Bequest (by exchange) and
Mrs. Marya Bernard Fund in memory of her hus-
band Dr. Bernard Bernard and anonymous funds

The Bull. *Paris, December 12, 1945–January 17, 1946*

If the Minotaur embodied the dangerous passions of the 1930s, the bulls of Picasso's postwar work have been reduced to domestic animals, stripped of mythological overtones, powerful but tame. Fernand Mourlot, the printer who assisted Picasso with this famous series of lithographs, remarked that he reworked the image like a butcher carving away slices of a carcass. It seems to bear out the artist's statement that "a picture used to be a sum of additions. In my case a picture is a sum of destructions." As Irving Lavin has pointed out, the possibility of striking prints from successive states of the same lithographic stone satisfied Picasso's long-standing desire to record the evolution of his own creative process. The evolution of *The Bull* begins with naturalistic images, passes through several stages of curvilinear Cubism, and concludes with a scrawled outline recalling the prehistoric drawings of bull-like creatures in the caves of Lascaux, discovered only five years earlier. It seems, in Lavin's words, like a demonstration of "art history in reverse." Even as he reduces the image, Picasso creates new relationships among its elements. The bull's tail, flicking forward in the second and third states, suggests an imaginary contour, descending from rump to foreleg, that persists even in the sixth state, where the tail hangs at rest. (It is now matched by a similar arc extending from head to hind leg.) In the final state, the contours of gorge and hindquarters extend without a break into fore and hind legs; parallel curves describe the corresponding limb in each pair. The order of anatomy gives way to the order of art. Picasso's visual deconstruction had been anticipated by the Dutch artist Theo van Doesburg, who, in a 1917 series of drawings, reduced a cow to a Mondrian-like arrangement of colored rectangles. In comparison, Picasso's lithograph seems less didactic—and far more evocative of the actual beast. P.K.

THE BULL (LE TAUREAU), state II. Paris, December 12, 1945
Lithograph, sheet: 13 × 16 ⅞" (33 × 42.9 cm)
Mourlot 17. Mrs. Gilbert W. Chapman Fund.

THE BULL (LE TAUREAU), state III. Paris, December 18, 1945
Lithograph, sheet: 13¼ × 20¼" (33.7 × 51.4 cm)
Mourlot 17. Mrs. Gilbert W. Chapman Fund

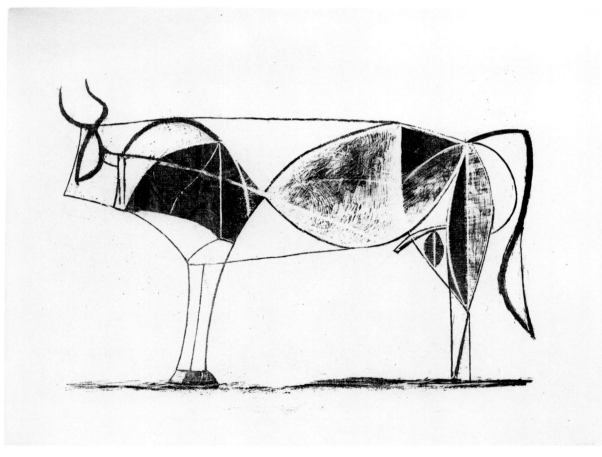

THE BULL (LE TAUREAU), state VI. Paris, December 26, 1945
Lithograph, sheet: 12⅞ × 17½" (32.7 × 44.5 cm)
Mourlot 17. Mrs. Gilbert W. Chapman Fund

THE BULL (LE TAUREAU), state VIII. Paris, January 2, 1946
Lithograph, sheet: 13 × 22" (33 × 55.9 cm)
Mourlot 17. Mrs. Gilbert W. Chapman Fund

THE BULL (LE TAUREAU), state VII, (counter proof). Paris, December 28, 1945
Lithograph, sheet: 15¾ × 20⁹⁄₁₆" (40 × 52.2 cm)
Mourlot 17. Mrs. Gilbert W. Chapman Fund

THE BULL (LE TAUREAU), state XI. Paris, January 17, 1946
Lithograph, sheet: 13 × 17½" (33 × 44.5 cm)
Mourlot 17. Acquired through the Lillie P. Bliss Bequest

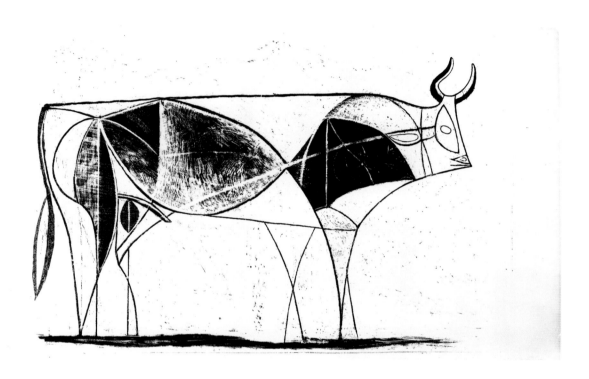

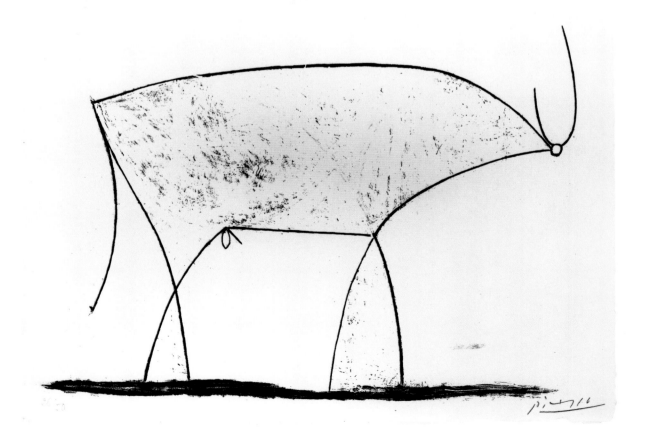

Woman in an Armchair. *Paris, December 30, 1948–January 16, 1949*

In 1943, Picasso met Françoise Gilot, a talented young artist who seemed to combine the sensual allure of Marie-Thérèse Walter with the challenging intelligence of Dora Maar. They began living together in 1946, and would separate seven years later. Gilot's 1964 memoir, *Life with Picasso*, chronicled their tumultuous relationship, but also revealed a surprisingly philosophical side to the artist's personality. The years immediately following the war marked a period of new political engagement for Picasso. France seemed polarized between the largely left-wing partisans of the Resistance and the discredited right-wingers who had collaborated with Germany. Picasso declared his sympathies by joining the Communist Party, despite its condemnation of "bourgeois" avant-garde art like his own. In August 1948, he participated in a "peace" conference in Poland, from which he brought back the embroidered jacket that Françoise wears in this *Woman in an Armchair*. The image began as an elaborate color lithograph, using five different plates to superimpose black lines on fields of yellow, red, green, and violet. Dissatisfied with the composite image, Picasso reworked each plate as an independent likeness, printed in black. Here, on what had been the red plate, he preserved the natural proportions of head and torso, but emphasized the puffy sleeves of the Polish jacket. In the intermediate stages, the image is decorated with spiky lines and serifs, but these vanish in the final state, replaced by baroque tendrils and a luminous, naturalistic face. The large, rounded forms recall Picasso's 1946 portrait of Françoise as a "Woman-flower," an image of hope regained after the long nightmare of the war. P.K.

WOMAN IN AN ARMCHAIR NO. 1 (FEMME AU FAUTEUIL NO.1), final state. Paris, December 30, 1948
Lithograph, comp.: 27 3/16 × 20 1/16" (69.0 × 51.0 cm)
Mourlot 134. Curt Valentin Bequest

Pregnant Woman. *Vallauris, 1950*

Françoise Gilot and Picasso had a son, Claude, in 1947, and a daughter, Paloma, in 1949. A year later, when Picasso voiced his wish that she have a third child, she declined. Not long after, he sculpted the *Pregnant Woman*. "I think this sculpture was a form of wish fulfillment," Gilot later commented. For several years, Picasso had been making and decorating ceramics in the traditional pottery center of Vallauris. He and Françoise moved to a nearby villa, and an old perfume factory became his studio, where both the *She-Goat* (plate, p. 129) and *Pregnant Woman* were created. The woman's distended breasts and abdomen were modeled around clay water pitchers that Picasso had rescued from a scrap heap. In contrast to the overall rough texture of the surface, the smooth, polished bronze in these areas gives the impression of skin stretched tight. Despite the sculpture's superficial naturalism, it seems to recall the grotesquely exaggerated proportions of prehistoric fertility goddesses like the Venus of Lespugue, a work much admired by the Surrealists. (Picasso owned two casts of it.) The woman's swollen torso teeters on sticklike legs, without any real feet to help her balance. Slightly taller than half life-size, she seems like some kind of totemic figure, a deity from Picasso's private mythology. P.K.

PREGNANT WOMAN. Vallauris, 1950
Bronze (cast 1955), 41¼ × 7⅝ × 6¼" (104.8 × 19.3 × 15.8 cm), including base. Spies 349
Gift of Mrs. Bertram Smith

She-Goat. *Vallauris, 1950*

Despite the privations of the war, Picasso kept his interest in sculpture alive during the 1940s. The one large figure he sculpted during the occupation, *Man with Sheep* (1943; Philadelphia Museum of Art), had a solemn, ritualistic air, with ambivalent overtones of both protection and sacrifice. This formidably vital *She-Goat*, however, belongs to a new burst of sculptural production at the start of the 1950s, and has a more heartily rude comic presence. It and related assemblage sculptures of the day have an improvisatory playfulness that may connect to Picasso's engagement with the two new children, Paloma and Claude, he fathered at the time with his mistress, Françoise Gilot. Picasso always had a great knack for spotting potential images, animal or otherwise, in pieces of scrap, pebbles, and so on—as is most famously shown in his splicing of a bicycle seat and handlebar to make a *Head of a Bull* in 1942 (Musée Picasso, Paris). Thus, when he established a new studio in the small potter's village of Vallauris in 1948, he kept a constant eye on the yard next door, where the town's broken ceramics, scrap metal, and other detritus accumulated, looking for accidental fragments that might spark some new idea. In this case, we know from Gilot that Picasso first conceived the idea of making a goat in sculpture, then set out to find the appropriate elements, which he then held together with plaster. The face and spine were fashioned from a large palm frond the artist had retrieved from the beach years before, the bony rib cage originated in an old wicker wastebasket, the horns were vine stalks, the legs were tree branches (with knots serving for joints in the hindquarters), and metal scraps were inserted into the haunches to make them appear properly bony. Picasso took particular care with, and delight in, the sexual markers and underbelly. He broke and reshaped milk pitchers to make the pendulous teats, then inserted a partially bent can top to make a prominent vulva, and between it and the tail set a protruding pipe to denote the anus. Goats were companions to the gamboling gods and nymphs in many of Picasso's postwar imaginings of arcadia, and he first cast this one in bronze so that it could be a constant presence in his garden—where it occasionally served as a hitching post for the actual goat he took on as a pet a few years later. Even in bronze, though, the separate pieces betray their makeshift origins, and add to the coarsely vivid character of this appealing animal. K.V.

SHE-GOAT. Vallauris, 1950
Bronze (cast 1952), after an assemblage of palm leaf, ceramic flowerpots, wicker basket, metal elements, and plaster, 46⅜ × 56⅜ × 28⅛" (117.7 × 143.1 × 71.4 cm), including base. Spies 409
Mrs. Simon Guggenheim Fund

Pablo Picasso
Spanish, 1881-1973
to France 1904

She-Goat 1950
Bronze (cast 1952) after an
assemblage of palm leaf,
ceramic flowerpots, wicker
basket, metal elements and
plaster.
Mrs. Simon Guggenheim Fund,
1959

Baboon and Young. *Vallauris, 1951*

Like the bronze *She-Goat* (previous page), *Baboon and Young* was cast from an assemblage of found objects united by plaster. The head consists of two toy cars that Daniel-Henry Kahnweiler had brought to Vallauris as presents for Picasso's son Claude; the ears were ceramic pitcher handles from a scrap heap; the shoulders were larger handles; as in the *Pregnant Women* (plate, p. 127), the bulging belly was a large pot. The transformation of car into head is particularly striking: the divided windshield becomes a pair of eye sockets, while the hood stretches out precisely like a muzzle. The metamorphoses of Picasso's sculptures are both humorous and alarming, subverting the stability of the everyday world with their open-ended "confusion of identity." The simian motif of the sculpture was also clearly important to Picasso. He kept a pet monkey for several years at the Bateau-Lavoir in Paris, and again in the late 1930s. His *saltimbanques* and lovers of the Blue Period had often been accompanied by watchful monkeys; indeed, no less a critic than Dora Maar later noted that his mannerist figures of this period (compare p. 35) possessed the elongated limbs and fingers of apes. In these early pictures, the monkey seemed like a symbol of untamable playfulness and freedom. When he returns, in a 1953–54 series of drawings contrasting a beautiful nude and her aged, melancholy suitors, he has acquired a new, ironic significance. As John Berger has noted, the young woman is amused by the monkey's ugliness and crude desires, while the same qualities in the aged man repel her. The baboon clutching a baby to its breast in Picasso's 1951 sculpture is clearly a female. Nonetheless, it seems like a disguised self-portrait, offering satiric expression to the desire for children that had also impelled the creation of the 1950 *Pregnant Woman*. P.K.

BABOON AND YOUNG. Vallauris, 1951
Bronze (cast 1955), after found objects, 21 × 13¼ × 20¾" (53.3 × 33.3 × 52.7 cm). Spies 463
Mrs. Simon Guggenheim Fund

Paloma and Her Doll on Black Background.

December 14, 1952

As in the *Two Nudes* of 1906 (plate, p. 45), Picasso's 1952 lithograph superimposes images of youth and maturity. His three year-old daughter Paloma cradles a doll in her lap, as if it were a child and she an adult. The uncanny self-possession of small children is translated here into a kind of regal dignity. But Paloma's rounded, cherubic face seems disturbingly at odds with her piercing eyes and sensual lips. Picasso's extraordinary graphic style, with its webs of lines terminated by crossbars like tiny nail heads, can be traced back to the semiabstract "constellations" found in his notebook drawings of 1924 (see p. 91). When this style returns, around 1948, it is accompanied by a kind of *horror vacui*, which increasingly impelled the artist to fill every available space with networks of parallel or radiating lines. If these lines derive from conventional cross-hatching, they have assumed an unprecedented independence, angling into space like the iron rods of the *Project for a Monument to Guillaume Apollinaire* (plate, p. 95). The task of shading usually assigned to cross-hatching is handled in this lithograph by a subtle alternation between areas of black on white and areas of white on black, with light and dark lines merging into a seemingly continuous web. Individual forms are sometimes reinforced and sometimes contradicted by the effects of shading. A spiral (recalling Picasso's favorite childhood pastry) evokes Paloma's rounded chin. But the concentric ovals of her cheek, at left, evoke a gash instead of a convex form. A kind of graphic scarification initiates her into the adult world of her father's art.   P.K.

PALOMA AND HER DOLL ON BLACK BACK-
GROUND (PALOMA À LA POUPÉE SUR FOND
NOIR). December 14, 1952
Lithograph, comp.: 27 ¹¹⁄₁₆ × 21¾" (70.4 × 55.3 cm)
Mourlot 229. Curt Valentin Bequest

133

Woman by a Window. *Cannes, June 1956*

Picasso's relationship with Françoise Gilot came apart in late 1952, around the same time that a young divorcée named Jacqueline Rocque came to work at one of the potteries in Vallauris. Jacqueline's command of Spanish gave her a natural avenue of contact with Picasso, and soon after Françoise left him definitively, at the start of 1953, Jacqueline took over as the woman in his life; they would be married in 1961. The advent of Jacqueline overlapped with the departure from Picasso's life of his great rival and perhaps only peer in modern painting, Henri Matisse, who died in November 1954. Feeling himself heir to Matisse's orientalizing tendencies, and spurred by what he saw as Jacqueline's resemblance to one of the women in Eugène Delacroix's *Les Femmes d'Alger (Women of Algiers)* of 1834, Picasso set out on a series of lavish remakings of Delacroix's harem composition in 1954 and 1955 (see fig. 7, p. 21). Some of that exoticism may persist in the rather hieratic presence of Jacqueline in this image, and certainly Matisse's ongoing presence is felt, especially in the scribed curves of the rocking chair in which she sits. The locale is the new villa, La Californie, that Picasso had taken in Cannes, and the arched window opens onto a palm in the tropical garden that was one of the property's prime attractions. The dark, shadowy cool of this studio, in contrast to the sunlit lushness beyond, became a frequent subject for the artist at this time, with or without the presence of a figure. Here, in keeping with the tautness of her almost Egyptian pose, Jacqueline seems to dominate our encounter with her through the frozen alertness in the gaze of her one giant, frontal eye. However, as William Rubin has remarked, her other, profile eye, in conjunction with the large triangle that projects from the picture on the easel between her and the window, suggests that another part of her consciousness is drawn to the art at hand, rather than to the artist who paints her. K.V.

WOMAN BY A WINDOW. Cannes, June 1956
Oil on canvas, 63¾ × 51¼" (162 × 130 cm)
Zervos XVII, 120. Mrs. Simon Guggenheim Fund

Bull. *Cannes, c. 1958*

In the early 1950s, the incorporation of real objects had impelled Picasso to make fully three-dimensional sculptures like *Pregnant Woman, She-Goat,* and *Baboon and Young* (plates, pp. 127, 129, 131). In contrast, his sculptures of the later 1950s were mostly flat figures constructed from boards and sticks. This formal vocabulary of planes and lines overlapping in a shallow space looked back more than forty years to the *papiers collés* of 1912 (see p. 67). While many of Picasso's sculptures of the late 1950s are severely rectilinear, the *Bull* is constructed from pine boards and plywood sheets cut into ovals and curves that recall the intermediate states of his 1945–46 *Bull* lithograph (plates, pp. 121–23). Lines are "drawn" across the surface with sticks, branches, and table legs—sometimes curved, sometimes straight. Dozens of tiny nails, hammered into the plywood, suggest the bull's shaggy coat. Within the same overall silhouette, each side of the *Bull* presents a different arrangement of lines and planes. On one side, a small picture frame, stripped of its canvas and mounted backwards on the plywood expanse of head, neck, and horns, represents the face. The eyes are indicated by two flathead nails flanking a rough wooden square, the nose by a carved wooden ball, the mouth by a gouge in the plywood. The manmade materials in this area contrast with the natural forms of the tree branches at left and right, as if to suggest the bull's double nature—half-wild, half-domesticated. P.K.

BULL. Cannes, c. 1958
Plywood, tree branch, nails, screws, 46⅛ × 56¾ × 4⅛" (117.2 × 144.1 × 10.5 cm). Spies 545
Gift of Jacqueline Picasso in honor of the Museum's continuous commitment to Pablo Picasso's art

Plate 1 *from the series* **347 Gravures.** *Mougins, 1968.*

Suite published Paris, 1968

Well past eighty years old, Picasso turned back to printmaking with a rejuvenated enthusiasm, spurred by his collaboration with two young printmakers, Aldo and Piero Crommelynck. At the end of 1968, he showed a group of 347 etchings he had executed, in an amazing burst of productivity, over a six-month period between March and October of that year. Gert Schiff called this suite of prints "the most comprehensive statement ever made by the artist about his philosophy of painting, and of life." In a broadly varied, virtually diaristic sequence of scenes from the studio, the circus, and the brothel, Picasso seems to have reviewed his life, or indeed life itself. He imagined himself in the guises of child, as activist artist hero, aging Silenus, and impotent, senescent voyeur, and revisited many of the themes, especially of creativity and eroticism, that had preoccupied him throughout his career. One constant in the whole array is the artist's stunning command of line and medium. Many have found in Picasso's paintings of this period signs of slackness or rote performance, but the taut energies and creative potency of these late graphic works seem incontestable, and remarkable. The first plate in the group, done over the week of March 16–22, is one of the most densely worked, and is remarkable for a very rare instance in which the artist depicted himself in recognizable, resembling terms, as a bald and wrinkled old man. Flanked behind by an austere, almost priestly figure who seems associated with Picasso's remembrances of Diego Velázquez's Spain, he faces—in the guise of a circus strong man—what appears to be one of his own avatars, the hirsute and hearty sculptor of 1930s imagery (see pp. 103, 106). Between them reclines a youth bathed in light—the fictive dreamer of the scene?—and above him unfolds a scene of equine acrobatics that looks back to Picasso's very early studies of circus riders (see p. 41). Emerging from the darkness beyond are an array of faces that recalls the rows of masks Picasso made as a theatrical backdrop for Jean Cocteau's 1922 staging of *Antigone*. The dark theatricality, and the specificity of self-reference, would be abandoned as Picasso moved forward with this suite of etchings, but the exaggerated voluptuousness of the acrobat, and the equally insisted-upon masculinity of her steed, offer a premonition of the pungent eroticism that would permeate this fervent, sometimes almost obsessive, graphic meditation on life seen from its waning end. K.V.

PLATE 1 from the series 347 GRAVURES.
Mougins, 1968

Etching, plate: 15½ × 22¼" (39.3 × 56.5 cm)
Geiser/Baer VI, 1496. Gift of the Bibliothèque
Nationale de France (by exchange)

At Work. *August 1971*

In the final decades of his life, increasingly isolated by fame, wealth, and age, Picasso found inspiration in a series of confrontations with the great masters of European painting, creating deeply personal reinterpretations of Diego Velázquez's *Meninas (Maids of Honor;* 1656), Eugène Delacroix's *Femmes d'Alger (Women of Algiers;* 1834), and Édouard Manet's *Le Dejeuner sur l'herbe (Luncheon on the Grass;* 1863). After a long illness in 1965–66, he turned to Rembrandt, depicting a series of musketeers whose broad-brimmed hats, embroidered tunics, neatly trimmed beards, and prominently flaunted swords recalled the swaggering burghers of *The Night Watch* (1642). As Gert Schiff noted, these musketeers often metamorphosed into painters, clutching paintbrushes instead of swords. In *At Work,* painted less than two years before his death (on April 8, 1973), Picasso endowed himself with the long hair and square-cornered tunic of his 1960s musketeers, but these dashing attributes were contradicted by the figure's squat proportions and oversized feet, which recall the sculpted baboon of 1951 (plate, p. 131) or the leering dwarves who often appear in his late drawings and prints, grotesque symbols of sexual frustration. The visual rhyme between Picasso's almond-shaped eyes, boldly confronting his own mortality, and the figure eight of his nostrils recalls numerous portraits of the late 1930s. What is new is the violence and expressiveness of the brushwork, boiling over in loops and slashes of green, pink, blue, and gray, beating against the thick black outlines of the figure, and exploding into a fan of black-and-white strokes at upper left. P.K.

AT WORK. August 1971

Oil on canvas, 63¾ × 51¼" (161.9 × 130.2 cm) Zervos XXXIII, 145. Gift of Jacqueline Picasso in honor of the Museum's continuous commitment to Pablo Picasso's art.

REFERENCES FOR WORKS OF ART

The following catalogues were used to identify works by Picasso, and are cited in abbreviated form throughout this volume.

D.B.
Pierre Daix and Georges Boudaille, with Joan Rosselet. *Picasso: The Blue and Rose Periods—A Catalogue Raisonné of the Paintings, 1900–1906.* Translated by Phoebe Pool. Greenwich, Conn.: New York Graphic Society, 1966. Originally published as *Picasso 1900–1906: Catalogue raisonné de l'oeuvre peint.* Neuchâtel: Ides and Calendes, 1966. *Note:* Citations in which a lowercase *d* precedes the volume number indicate the catalogued drawings of Picasso, as opposed to the paintings.

D.R.
Pierre Daix and Joan Rosselet. *Picasso: The Cubist Years, 1907–1916—A Catalogue Raisonné of the Paintings and Related Works.* Translated by Dorothy S. Blair. Boston: New York Graphic Society; London: Thames and Hudson, 1979. Originally published as *Le Cubisme de Picasso: Catalogue raisonné de l'oeuvre peint, 1907–1916.* Neuchätel: Ides and Calendes, 1979.

GEISER/BAER
Picasso, peintre-graveur. Vol. I, by Bernhard Geiser (Bern: B. Geiser, 1933); updated by Brigitte Baer (Bern: Kornfeld, 1990). Vol. II, by Geiser (Bern: Kornfeld and Klipstein, 1968); updated by Baer (Bern: Editions Kornfeld, 1992). Vols. III-VII and Addenda, by Baer (Bern: Editions Kornfeld, 1986–96).

MOURLOT
Fernand Mourlot. *Picasso Lithographs.* Boston: Boston Book and Art Publisher, 1970. Originally published as *Picasso lithographe, 1919–1963.* 4 vols., Monte-Carlo: André Sauret, Éditions du Livre, 1949–64. Reprinted 1970.

P.P.
Herschel Chipp and Alan Wofsy. *The Picasso Project: Picasso's Paintings, Watercolors, Drawings, and Sculpture—A Comprehensive Illustrated Catalogue, 1885–1973.* San Francisco: Alan Wofsy Fine Arts, 1995–97. *From Cubism to Neoclassicism, 1917–1919* (1995). *Neoclassicism I, 1920–1921* (1995). *Neoclassicism II, 1922–1924* (1996). *Toward Surrealism, 1925–1929* (1996). *Surrealism, 1930–1936* (1997).

RICHET
Michèle Richet. *Musée Picasso: Catalogue sommaire des collections, vol. II: Dessins, aquarelles, gouaches, pastels.* Paris: Ministère de la Culture et de la Communication, Editions de la Rèunion des musées nationaux, 1987.

SPIES
Werner Spies. *Picasso: Das plastische Werk.* Stuttgart: Verlag Gerd Hatje, 1983.

ZERVOS
Christian Zervos. *Pablo Picasso.* 33 vols. Paris: Cahiers d'art, 1932–78.

NOTE:
Photographic reproductions of unpublished works from the Estate of Pablo Picasso (Picasso Succession) can be consulted at the Musée Picasso, Paris, where they are catalogued by inventory number.

BIBLIOGRAPHY

The following principal reference sources are cited in abbreviated form in the notes to the catalogue entries.

ADAMS 1980
Brooks Adams, "Picasso's Absinthe Glasses: Six Drinks to the End of an Era." *Artforum* (New York) 18, no. 8 (April 1980), pp. 30–33.

APOLLINAIRE 1913
Guillaume Apollinaire. "Picasso and the *Papiers Collés.*" *Montjoie!*, March 14, 1913. Translated in Leroy C. Breunig, ed. *Apollinaire on Art, Essays and Reviews 1902–1918.* New York: The Viking Press, 1972.

ARAGON 1930
Louis Aragon. "Challenge to Painting" (1930). Introduction to *Exposition de Collage.* Paris: Galerie Goemans, Librairie José Corti, 1930. Translated by Lucy R. Lippard, in Lippard, ed. *Surrealists on Art.* Englewood Cliffs, N.J.: Prentice-Hall, 1970.

BAER 1984
Brigitte Baer, cited in Marilyn August. "Brigitte Baer: A New Perspective on Picasso" [interview]. *ArtNews* (New York) 83, no. 3 (March 1984), p. 77.

BARR 1946
Alfred H. Barr, Jr. *Picasso: Fifty Years of His Art.* New York: The Museum of Modern Art, 1946. Reprinted, 1974.

BARR-SCHARRAR 1972
Beryl Barr-Sharrar. "Some Aspects of Early Autobiographical Imagery in Picasso's *Suite 347.*" *The Art Bulletin* (New York) 54, no. 4 (December 1972), pp. 516–33.

BERGER 1965
John Berger. *The Success and Failure of Picasso.* Harmondsworth: Penguin, 1965. Reprinted New York: Pantheon, 1980.

BLUNT/POOL 1962
Anthony Blunt and Phoebe Pool. *Picasso: The Formative Years—A Study of His Sources.* London: Studio Books, 1962.

BOGGS 1992
Jean Sutherland Boggs. *Picasso and Things.* With essays by Marie-Laure Bernadac and Brigitte Léal. Cleveland: The Cleveland Museum of Art, 1992.

BOIS 1987
Yve-Alain Bois. "Kahnweiler's Lesson." *Representations* (Berkeley, Calif.), no. 18 (Spring 1987), pp. 33–68. Revised text published in Bois, *Painting as Model.* Cambridge, Mass.: MIT Press, 1990.

BOIS 1992
Yve-Alain Bois. "The Semiology of Cubism." In William Rubin, Kirk Varnedoe, and Lynn Zelevansky, eds. *Picasso and Braque: A Symposium.* New York: The Museum of Modern Art, 1992.

BOLLIGER 1956
Hans Bolliger. *Picasso's Vollard Suite.* Translated by Norbert Guterman. London: Thames and Hudson, 1956. Reprinted, 1977. Revised and expanded, 1985; reprinted, 1994. Originally published as *Suite Vollard.* Stuttgart: Verlag Gerd Hatje, 1956.

BOWNESS 1973
Alan Bowness. "Picasso's Sculpture." In Roland Penrose and John Golding, eds. *Picasso in Retrospect.* New York: Praeger, 1973.

BRASSAÏ 1966
Brassaï. *Picasso and Company.* Translated by Francis Price. Garden City, N.Y.: Doubleday, 1966. Originally published as *Conversations avec Picasso.* Paris: Gallimard, 1964.

BURGARD 1986
Timothy Anglin Burgard. "Picasso's 'Night Fishing at Antibes': Autobiography, Apocalypse, and the Spanish Civil War." *The Art Bulletin* (New York) 68, no. 4 (December 1986), pp. 657–72.

BURGARD 1991
Timothy Anglin Burgard. "Picasso and Appropriation." *The Art Bulletin* (New York) 73, no. 3, (September 1991), pp. 479–94.

CARLSON 1976
Victor I. Carlson. *Picasso: Drawings and Watercolors, 1899–1907, in the Collection of the Baltimore Museum of Art.* Baltimore: The Baltimore Museum of Art, 1976.

CARMEAN 1980
E. A. Carmean, Jr. *Picasso: The Saltimbanques.* Washington, D.C.: National Gallery of Art, 1980.

CHIPP 1973
Herschel B. Chipp. "Guernica: Love, War, and the Bullfight." *Art Journal* (New York) 33, no. 2 (Winter 1973–74), pp. 100–15.

COOPER 1968
Douglas Cooper. *Picasso Theater.* New York: Harry N. Abrams, 1968. Originally published as *Picasso: Théâtre.* Paris: Cercle d'art, 1967

COUSINS 1989
Judith Cousins, with the collaboration of Pierre Daix. "Documentary Chronology." In William Rubin. *Picasso and Braque: Pioneering Cubism.* New York: The Museum of Modern Art, 1989.

DAIX 1993A
Pierre Daix. *Picasso: Life and Art.* Translated by

Olivia Emmet. New York: Harper-Collins, Icon Editions, 1993. Originally published as *Picasso créateur: La Vie intime et l'oeuvre*. Paris: Seuil, 1987.

DAIX 1993B
Pierre Daix. "Picasso at Auschwitz." *ArtNews* (New York) 92, no. 9 (September 1993), pp. 198–99.

DUFOUR 1969
Pierre Dufour. *Picasso, 1950–1968*. Geneva: Skira, 1969.

DOCUMENTS
Paris: Jean-Michel Place, 1991. 2 vols. Reprint of periodical originally published in Paris by Georges Bataille, 1929–30.

FITZGERALD 1987
Michael FitzGerald. *Pablo Picasso's Monument to Guillaume Apollinaire: Surrealism and Monumental Sculpture in France, 1918-1959*. Ph.D. dissertation, Columbia University, New York, 1987.

FITZGERALD 1995
Michael C. FitzGerald. *Making Modernism: Picasso and the Creation of the Market for Twentieth-century Art*. New York: Farrar, Straus and Giroux, 1995.

FLUEGEL 1980
Jane Fluegel. "Chronology." In William Rubin, ed. *Pablo Picasso: A Retrospective*. New York: The Museum of Modern Art, 1980.

GALASSI 1984
Susan Grace Galassi. "Lasting Impressions." *ArtNews* (New York) 83, no. 3 (May 1984), pp. 74–78.

GASMAN 1981
Lydia Gasman. "Mystery, Magic and Love in Picasso, 1925–1938: Picasso and the Surrealist Poets." Ph.D. dissertation, Columbia University, New York, 1981.

GILMOUR 1987
Pat Gilmour. "Picasso & His Printers." *The Print Collector's Newsletter* (New York) 18, no. 3 (July–August 1987), pp. 81–90.

GILOT/LAKE 1964
Françoise Gilot and Carlton Lake. *Life with Picasso*. New York: McGraw-Hill, 1964.

GOLDING 1988
John Golding. *Cubism: A History and an Analysis, 1907–1914*. Cambridge, Mass.: Harvard University Press, 1988. Originally published New York: Wittenborn, 1959.

GONZALEZ 1936
Julio Gonzalez. "Picasso sculpteur." *Cahiers d'art* (Paris) 11, nos. 6–7 (936), pp. 189–91.

GREENBERG 1966
Clement Greenberg. "Picasso Since 1945." *Artforum* (New York) 5, no. 2 (October 1966), pp. 28–31. Reprinted in John O'Brian, ed. *Clement*

Greenberg: The Collected Essays and Criticism, Volume 4: Modernism with a Vengeance, 1957–1969. Chicago: The University of Chicago Press, 1993.

HOOG 1988
Michel Hoog. *Les Grandes Baigneuses de Picasso*. Paris: Réunion des musées nationaux, 1988.

JAFFÉ 1983
H. L. C. Jaffé. *Theo van Doesburg*. Amsterdam: Menlenhoff/Landshoff, 1983.

JOHNSON 1976
Ron Johnson. *The Early Sculpture of Picasso, 1901-1914*. New York and London: Garland, 1976.

JOHNSON 1977A
Ronald Johnson. "Picasso's Parisian Family and the 'Saltimbanques.'" *Arts* (New York) 51, no. 5 (January 1977), pp. 90–95.

JOHNSON 1977B
Ronald Johnson. "Picasso's Musical and Mallarméan Constructions." *Arts* (New York) 51, no. 7 (March 1977), pp. 122–27.

JOHNSON 1980
Ron Johnson. "Picasso's 'Demoiselles d'Avignon' and the Theatre of the Absurd." *Arts* (New York) 55, no. 2 (October 1980), pp. 102–13.

KAHNWEILER 1949A
Daniel-Henry Kahnweiler. *The Sculptures of Picasso*. Translated by A. D. B. Sylvester. London: Rodney Phillips, 1949. Originally published as *Les Sculptures de Picasso*. Paris: Les Éditions du Chêne, 1948.

KAHNWEILER 1949B
Daniel-Henry Kahnweiler. *The Rise of Cubism*. New York: Wittenborn, Schultz, 1949. Originally published as *Der Weg zum Kubismus*, by Daniel Henry [pseud.]. Munich: Delphin, 1920.

KARMEL 1992
Pepe Karmel. "Notes on the Dating of Works." In William Rubin, Kirk Varnedoe, and Lynn Zelevansky, eds. *Picasso and Braque: A Symposium*. New York: The Museum of Modern Art, 1992.

KARMEL 1993
Pepe Karmel. "Picasso's Laboratory: The Role of His Drawings in the Development of Cubism, 1910–14." Doctoral thesis, Institute of Fine Arts, New York University, 1993.

KARMEL 1994
Pepe Karmel. "Beyond the 'Guitar': Painting, Drawing and Construction, 1912–14." In Elizabeth Cowling and John Golding, eds. *Picasso: Sculptor/Painter*. London: Tate Gallery, 1994.

KING 1987
Antoinette King. "The Conservation Treatment of a Collage: 'Man with a Hat' by Pablo Picasso." In Guy Petherbridge, ed. *Conservation of Library and Archive Materials and the Graphic Arts*. London: Butterworth's, 1987.

KRAUSS 1980
Rosalind Krauss. "Re-Presenting Picasso." *Art in America* (New York) 68, no. 10 (December 1980), pp. 90–96.

LAPORTE 1975
Geneviève Laporte, with annotations by Douglas Cooper. *Sunshine at Midnight: Memories of Picasso and Cocteau*. Translated by Douglas Cooper. New York: Macmillan, 1975. Originally published as *"Si tard le soir, le soleil brille. . . ": Pablo Picasso*. Paris: Plon, 1973.

LAVIN 1993
Irving Lavin. "Picasso's Bull(s): Art History in Reverse." *Art in America* (New York) 81, no. 3 (March 1993), pp. 76–93.

LÉAL 1996
Brigitte Léal. *Musée Picasso: Carnets—catalogue des dessins*. 2 vols. Paris: Réunion des Musées Nationaux, 1996.

LICHTENSTERN 1988
Christa Lichtenstern. *Pablo Picasso: Denkmal für Apollinaire: Entwurf zur Humanisierung des Raumes*. Frankfurt: Fischer, 1988.

LOMAS 1993
David Lomas. "A Canon of Deformity: 'Les Demoiselles d'Avignon' and Physical Anthropology." *Art History* (Oxford, U.K., and Cambridge, Mass.) 16, no. 3 (September 1993), pp. 424–46.

LORD 1993
James Lord. *Picasso and Dora: A Personal Memoir*. New York: Farrar Strauss Giroux, 1993.

MALRAUX 1976
André Malraux. *Picasso's Mask*. Translated by June Guicharnaud, with Jacques Guicharnaud. New York: Holt, Rinehart and Winston, 1976. Originally published as *La Tête d'obsidienne*. Paris: Gallimard, 1974.

MARRINAN 1977
Michael Marrinan. "Picasso as an 'Ingres' Young Cubist," *Burlington Magazine* (London) 119, no. 896 (November 1977), pp. 756–63.

MAYER 1979
Susan Mayer. "Greco-Roman and Egyptian Sources in Picasso's Blue Period." *Arts* (New York) 53 (June 1979), pp. 132–34.

MELVILLE 1942
Robert Melville. "Picasso in the Light of Chirico—Mutations of the Bullfight." *View* (New York) 1, no. 11 (February–March 1942), p. 2. Reprinted in Schiff 1976, pp. 90–93.

OLIVIER 1965
Fernande Olivier. *Picasso and His Friends*. Translated by Jane Miller. New York: Appleton-Century, 1965. Originally published as *Picasso et ses amis*. Paris: Librairie Stock Delamain et Boutelleau, 1933.

PENROSE 1958
Roland Penrose. *Picasso: His Life and Work.* London: Granada, 1981. Originally published London: Gollancz, 1958.

PENROSE 1967
Roland Penrose. *The Sculpture of Picasso.* New York: The Museum of Modern Art, 1967.

READ 1995
Peter Read. *Picasso et Apollinaire: Les Métamorphoses de la mémoire, 1905/1973.* Paris: Jean-Michel Place, 1995.

REFF 1971
Theodore Reff. "Harlequins, Saltimbanques, Clowns, and Fools." *Artforum* (New York) 10, no. 2 (October 1971), pp. 30–43.

REFF 1980
Theodore Reff. "Picasso's Three Musicians: Maskers, Artists and Friends." *Art in America* (New York) 68, no. 10 (December 1980), pp. 124–42.

RICHARDSON 1991
John Richardson, with Marilyn McCully. *A Life of Picasso, Volume I: 1881–1906.* New York: Random House, 1991.

RICHARDSON 1996
John Richardson, with Marilyn McCully. *A Life of Picasso, Volume II: 1907–1917.* New York: Random House, 1996.

RIES 1972
Martin Ries. "Picasso and the Myth of the Minotaur." *Art Journal* (New York) 32, no. 2 (Winter 1972–73), pp. 142–45.

ROSENBLUM 1983
Robert Rosenblum. "Notes on Picasso's Sculpture." *Art News* (New York) 82, no. 1 (January 1983), pp. 60–66.

ROSENBLUM 1996
Robert Rosenblum. "Picasso's Blond Muse: The Reign of Marie-Thérèse Walter." In William Rubin, ed. *Picasso and Portraiture: Representation and Transformation.* New York: The Museum of Modern Art, 1996.

ROSENTHAL 1983
Mark Rosenthal. "Picasso's 'Night Fishing at Antibes': A Meditation on Death." *The Art Bulletin* (New York) 65, no. 4 (December 1983), pp. 649–58.

RUBIN 1972
William Rubin. *Picasso in the Collection of The Museum of Modern Art.* New York: The Museum of Modern Art, 1972.

RUBIN 1980
William Rubin, ed. *Pablo Picasso: A Retrospective.* New York: The Museum of Modern Art, 1980.

RUBIN 1983
William Rubin. "From Narrative to 'Iconic' in Picasso: The Buried Allegory in 'Bread and Fruitdish on a Table' and the Role of 'Les Demoiselles d'Avignon.'" *The Art Bulletin* (New York) 65, no. 4 (December 1983), pp. 615–49.

RUBIN 1984
William Rubin. "Picasso." In Rubin, ed. *"Primitivism" in 20th Century Art: Affinity of the Tribal and the Modern.* Vol. I. New York: The Museum of Modern Art, 1984.

RUBIN 1989
William Rubin. *Picasso and Braque: Pioneering Cubism.* New York: The Museum of Modern Art, 1989.

RUBIN 1994
William Rubin. The Genesis of 'Les Demoiselles d'Avignon.'" In Rubin, ed. *Les Demoiselles d'Avignon.* Studies in Modern Art, no. 3. New York: The Museum of Modern Art, 1994. Adapted from "La Genèse des Demoiselles d'Avignon." In Hélène Seckel, ed. *Les Demoiselles d'Avignon.* 2 vols. Paris: Réunion des Musées Nationaux, 1988.

RUBIN 1996
William Rubin. "Reflections on Picasso and Portraiture." In Rubin, ed. *Picasso and Portraiture: Representation and Transformation.* New York: The Museum of Modern Art, 1996.

RUBIN/ARMSTRONG 1992
William Rubin and Matthew Armstrong. *The William S. Paley Collection.* New York: The Museum of Modern Art, 1992.

SABARTÉS 1948
Jaime Sabartés. *Picasso: An Intimate Portrait.* Translated by Angel Flores. New York: Prentice-Hall, 1948. Originally published as *Picasso: Portraits et Souvenirs.* Paris: Louis Carré and Maximilien Vox, 1946.

SCHIFF 1972
Gert Schiff. "Picasso's Suite 347, or Painting as an Act of Love." In Thomas B. Hess and Linda Nochlin, eds. *Woman as Sex Object.* New York: Newsweek, Inc., 1972. Reprinted in Schiff 1976, pp. 163–67.

SCHIFF 1976
Gert Schiff, ed. *Picasso in Perspective.* Englewood Cliffs, N.J.: Prentice-Hall, 1976.

SCHWARZ 1988
Herbert T. Schwarz. *Picasso and Marie-Thérèse Walter, 1925–1927.* Inuvik: Éditions Isabeau, 1988.

SECKLER 1947
Jerome Seckler. "Picasso Explains." *New Masses* Magazine (New York) 54, no. 11 (March 13, 1945), pp. 4–7.

SPIES 1981
Werner Spies, ed. *Pablo Picasso: Eine Austellung zum hundertsten Geburtstag; Werke aus der Sammlung Marina Picasso.* Munich: Prestel-Verlag, 1981.

STEIN 1933
Gertrude Stein. *The Autobiography of Alice B. Toklas.* New York: Harcourt, Brace, 1933. Reprinted New York: Modern Library, 1993.

STEIN 1938
Gertrude Stein. *Picasso.* London: B. T. Batsford, 1938. Reprinted New York: Dover, 1984. Originally published Paris: Floury, 1938.

STEINBERG 1968
Leo Steinberg. "Picasso's Sleepwatchers." *Life* (New York), December 27, 1968. Reprinted in Steinberg 1972, pp. 93–114.

STEINBERG 1971
Leo Steinberg. "Picasso: Drawing As If to Possess." *Artforum* (New York) 10, no. 2 (October 1971), pp. 44–53. Version published in Steinberg 1972, pp. 68–92.

STEINBERG 1972
Leo Steinberg. "The Algerian Women and Picasso at Large." In Steinberg. *Other Criteria: Confrontations with Twentieth-century Art.* London; Oxford, U.K.; and New York: Oxford University Press, 1972.

STEINBERG 1978
Leo Steinberg. "Resisting Cézanne: Picasso's 'Three Women.'" *Art in America* (New York) 66, no. 6 (November–December 1978), pp. 115–33.

STEINBERG 1979
Leo Steinberg. "The Polemical Part." *Art in America* (New York) 67, no. 2 (March–April 1979), pp. 115–27. Continuation of Steinberg 1978.

SWEENEY 1934
James Johnson Sweeney. *Plastic Redirections in 20th-century Painting.* Chicago: University of Chicago Press, 1934.

SWEENEY 1941
James Johnson Sweeney. "Picasso and Iberian Sculpture." *The Art Bulletin* (New York) 23, no. 3 (September 1941), pp. 191–99.

TUCKER 1970
William Tucker. "Four Sculptors, Part 2: Picasso Cubist Constructions." *Studio* (London) 179 (May 1970), pp. 201–05.

VARNEDOE 1995
Kirk Varnedoe. *Masterworks from the Louise Reinhardt Smith Collection.* New York: The Museum of Modern Art, 1995.

WITHERS 1978
Josephine Withers. *Julio González: Sculpture in Iron.* New York: New York University Press, 1978.

p. 32. *Meditation (Contemplation).* Paris, late 1904

D.B. XI, 12. Carlson 1976, fig. 2. Mayer 1979, pp. 136–37. Rubin 1972, pp. 30–31, 191. Steinberg 1968, pp. 93–95. Zervos I, 235.

p. 34. *The Frugal Repast.* Paris, September 1904

Baer 1984, p. 77. Barr 1946, pp. 29, 31, 49. Berger 1965, p. 42. Blunt/Pool 1962, p. 6, and n. to illus. 51. Brassaï 1966, p. 143. Geiser/Baer I, 2. Gilmour 1987, p. 82. Olivier 1965, pp. 27–28, 139. Penrose 1958, pp. 100–01, 129. Rubin 1972, pp. 28–30.

p. 36. *The Jester.* Paris, 1905

Barr 1946, p. 38. Blunt/Pool 1962, pp. 15–17, nos. 151–52, 157–59. D.B. XII, 21, 25. Johnson 1976, pp. 7–11, 26, 30–35. Kahnweiler 1949A, n.p. Olivier, pp. 33–34, 58–61, 143–44. Penrose 1958, pp. 76–77, 86–87. Penrose 1967, p. 17. Reff 1971, pp. 37, 42. Richardson 1991, pp. 203–07, 348–49, 456–57. Spies 4. Varnedoe 1995, p. 54. Zervos XXII, 206–09, 211, 215–17.

p. 38. *The Acrobats.* Paris, 1905

Blunt/Pool 1962, pp. 13, 26. Carlson 1976, pp. 24–25. Carmean 1980, pp. 29–32. D.B., XII, 17, and p. 255. Geiser/Baer I, 9. Johnson 1977A, p. 93. Olivier 1965, pp. 73, 127. Penrose 1958, p. 109. Reff 1971, *passim*.

p. 40. *Circus Rider.* Paris, 1905

D.B. XI, 18, 19; d.XII, 12–17. Reff 1971, p. 36. Rubin 1972, p. 34. Zervos XXII, 253–57.

p. 42. *Boy Leading a Horse.* Paris, 1905–06

Blunt/Pool 1962, pp. 26–27; figs. 162–66. Carmean 1980, pp. 55–56. D.B. XII, 33, 35; d.XII, 12–17; XIV, 3–16; d.XIV, 1. Geiser/Baer I, 10–11. Rubin 1972, pp. 34–35, 192–93. Rubin/Armstrong 1992, pp. 93–103, 165–68. Zervos I, 118, 264; XXII, 253, 256.

p. 44. *Two Nudes.* Paris, late 1906

Barr 1946, p. 52. Blunt/Pool 1962, n. to figs. 109–10. D.B. VII, 22; d.VII, 4, 6; XV, 6–12; XVI, 15. D.R. 101–04, 126–28. Léal 1996, vol. I, cat. 6, sheet 45R. Lomas 1993, pp. 424–46. Lord 1993, p. 150. Marrinan 1977, p. 756. Mayer 1979, pp. 132–34. Rubin 1972, p. 38. Rubin 1984, pp. 247–48. Sweeney 1941, pp. 195–96, and *passim*. Zervos I, 356–61, 366.

p. 46. *Head of a Sleeping Woman.* Paris, summer 1907

Barr 1946, pp. 59–60, 249. Daix 1993A, p. 74. D.R. 53–54, 78–85, 92–95. Gilot/Lake 1964, pp. 75–76. Golding 1988, pp. 43–45. Kahnweiler 1949B, p. 7. Léal 1996, vol. I, nos. 11, 12. Rubin 1984, pp. 254–55, 266–67. Rubin 1994, pp. 120–21. Sweeney 1934, pp. 17–19. Zervos II*, 5,

44, and p. 10; II**, 671–76; XXVI, 141, 162–65, 195–221.

p. 48. *Fruit Dish.* Paris, winter 1908–09

Barr 1946, p. 65. D.R. 210. Penrose 1958, pp. 142–43. Rubin 1972, pp. 54–55, 201. Rubin 1983, pp. 619–22. Zervos II*, 121, 122, 124, 126; VI, 1076; XXVI, 377.

p. 50. *Bather.* Paris, 1908–09

D.R. 239. Marrinan 1977, p. 756. Richardson 1996, pp. 108–09. Steinberg 1971, pp. 51–52, and *passim*. Steinberg 1978, p. 125. Steinberg 1979, pp. 115–19. Succession nos. 1189–1192. Varnedoe 1995, p. 32. Zervos II*, 110, 111; VI, 930, 1113; XXVI, 368–71.

p. 52. *Head.* Paris, spring 1909

Barr 1946, p. 66. D.R. 134–53, 259–69. Kahnweiler 1949A, n.p. Zervos II*, 148; II**, 713; VI, 1119; XXVI, 407, 410.

p. 54. *Woman's Head (Fernande).* Paris, fall 1909

Barr 1946, p. 69. D.R. 300–02. Gonzalez 1936, p. 189; cited in Penrose 1958, pp. 239–40, and Bowness 1973, p. 130. Kahnweiler 1949A, n.p. Penrose 1958, p. 146. Richardson 1996, pp. 123–28, 138–41. Stein 1933, p. 23. Stein 1938, p. 9. Spies 24, and pp. 47–54. Succession no. 1190. Zervos XXVI, 26, 397, 398, 413, 414, 417.

p. 56. *Still Life with Liqueur Bottle.* Horta de Ebro, August 1909

D.R. 274–303. Olivier 1965, pp. 132–37. Richardson 1996, pp. 128–35, 140–42. Rubin 1972, pp. 62, 204. Zervos II*, 173.

p. 58. *Girl with a Mandolin (Fanny Tellier).* Paris, 1910

Barr 1946, pp. 66, 70. D.R. 346. Gilot/Lake 1964, p. 119. Penrose 1958, pp. 155–56. Rubin 1972, pp. 66–67, 205. Zervos II*, 235.

p. 60. *The Architect's Table.* Paris, early 1912

Boggs 1992, nos. 96–97. Bois 1992, p. 171. Cousins 1989, p. 389. D.R. 456. Musée Picasso archival photograph no. 110. Rubin 1972, p. 72. Stein 1933, p. 111. Zervos II*, 321.

p. 62. *Standing Nude.* 1912

Bois 1987, *passim*. Bois 1992, pp. 187–90. Brassaï 1966, pp. 162–63. Cousins 1989, pp. 383–401. Kahnweiler 1949A, n.p. Krauss 1980, pp. 93–94. Steinberg 1972, pp. 165–66. Zervos II**, 392; XXVIII, 38, 129, 166.

p. 64. Maquette for *Guitar.* Paris, October 1912

Cousins 1989, p. 407. D.R. 488, 489. Johnson 1977A, pp. 122–24. Kahnweiler 1949A, n.p. Karmel 1994, pp. 189–92. Olivier 1965, p. 125. Rubin 1989, pp. 30–35. Spies 27A. Zervos II**, 392, 760, 761, 763; XXVIII, 198.

p. 66. *Man with a Hat.* Paris, December 1912

Apollinaire 1913; cited in Schiff 1976, pp. 51–52. Aragon 1930, pp. 38–40. D.R. 534, 537, 538. Gilot/Lake 1946, pp. 119–20. Karmel 1993, pp. 202–04. King 1987, *passim*. Zervos II**, 387, 398, 747, 748; XXVIII, 87.

p. 68. *Glass, Guitar, and Bottle.* Paris, early 1913

D.R. 564–70. Kahnweiler 1949A, n.p. Karmel 1994, pp. 189–92. Rubin 1972, pp. 80–81, 210. Zervos II**, 419.

p. 70. *Card Player.* Paris, winter 1913–14

Barr 1946, p. 83. D.R. 538, 650. Gilot/Lake 1964, pp. 119–20. Olivier 1965, pp. 58, 123–24. Rubin 1972, pp. 86, 211. Zervos II**, 466; XXIX, 8.

p. 72. *Student with Pipe.* Paris, March 1914

Cousins 1989, p. 425. D.R. 620, 621, 646, 783. Karmel 1992, pp. 337–39. Penrose 1958, pp. 181–82. Richardson 1996, p. 291. Richet 355. Zervos II**, 444, 840; VI, 1170, 1171, 1179; XXIX, 70, 92, 93.

p. 74. *Green Still Life.* Avignon, summer 1914

Barr 1946, pp. 90–91. D.R. 778. Rubin 1972, pp. 94–95, 213. Zervos II**, 485.

p. 76. *Glass of Absinthe.* Paris, spring 1914

Adams 1980, *passim*. Barr 1946, pp. 90–91. Boggs 1992, nos. 49–50. D.R. 753–58. Johnson 1977B, p. 125. Kahnweiler 1949A, n.p. Penrose 1958, p. 179. Penrose 1967, p. 20. Rubin 1972, pp. 95, 213. Spies 36D. Zervos II**, 579–584.

p. 78. *Two Dancers.* Summer 1919

FitzGerald 1995, pp. 92–93. Penrose 1958, pp. 195–201. P.P. 19.211. Rubin 1972, pp. 108, 217. Zervos III, 338–45; IV, 380; XXIX, 301, 375, 408–11, 430, 414, 415, 432, 425, 426, 551.

p. 80. *Three Musicians.* Fontainebleau, summer 1921

Cooper 1967, nos. 129–31, 237–40, 259–62, 283. FitzGerald 1995, pp. 92–93. Penrose 1958, p. 108. P.P. 21.259. Reff 1980, *passim*. Rubin 1972, pp. 112–14, 218–19. Zervos II**, 893, 894; III, 135, 193–97; IV, 331; XXIX, 240.

p. 82. *Nude Seated on a Rock.* Fontainebleau, summer 1921

FitzGerald 1995, pp. 106–09. Gilot/Lake 1964, pp. 20, 119. Hoog 1988, *passim*. Elaine L. Johnson, in Rubin 1972, p. 117. Penrose 1958, pp. 219–20. P.P. 21.254. Zervos IV, 309.

p. 84. *Studio with Plaster Head.* Juan-les-Pins, summer 1925

Barr 1946, pp. 122–23. Boggs 1992, no. 86. Cooper 1967, p. 66. Léal 1996, vol. I, pp. 26–27, 39–41. P.P. 25.086. Rubin 1972, pp. 120–22. Zervos V, 364, 372, 375–77, 380, 442, 444, 445, 451; VI, 1337.

p. 86. *Seated Woman.* Paris, 1927

Barr 1946, pp. 132–133, 146–148. Cooper 1968, pp. 41, 44, 45, 55–61; figs. 129–131, 237–240, 283, 331–332, 340–342, 349. *Documents*, pp. 135, 173. FitzGerald 1995, pp. 137–141. Geiser/Baer I, 84, 87, 88, 90–95, 213, 214, 241, 242. Léal 1996, vol. I, pp. 341–44. Léal 1996, vol. II, pp. 25–28; carnet 28, sheets 68–70, 84–87; carnet 29, sheets 1–6, 16–25; carnet 31, sheets 4, 13–16, 26–30; carnet 32, sheets 35, 38–41; carnet 33, sheets 3–4, 36, 45, 46, 51; carnet 34, sheet 19. Penrose 1958, pp. 36, 215–16. Picasso Estate Inventory, nos. 1070V, 1189, 1190, 1191, 1192. P.P. 27.016. Richet 498, 499, 500–14, 653–62. Rubin 1972, pp. 124–25, 223. Rubin 1996, pp. 60–63. Schwartz 1988, pp. 53–57, and *passim*. Spies 17. Steinberg 1972, pp. 193–94. Zervos III, 18, 21, 23, 49, 88, 90–95, 151, 201–02; V, 189–95, 198–99, 269–72, 274; VI, 924, 930, 931, 932, 939, 940, 948, 949, 964, 965, 972, 973, 1048, 1049, 1113, 1344; VII, 1, 2, 4–8, 11, 16, 22, 23, 30, 31, 38–41, 60, 76, 77, 81, 237; XXVI, 176, 181–83, 185, 244; XXIX, 287, 303, 304, 316, 318, 321, 322, 323.

p. 88. *Painter and Model Knitting.* Paris, late 1927

Barr 1946, pp. 144–45. Bolliger 1956, pp. v–x. FitzGerald 1987, pp. 80–189. Fluegel 1980, p. 253. Geiser/Baer I, 126. Penrose 1958, pp. 238–39, 268.

p. 90. *Guitars.* Juan-les-Pins, 1924

Barr 1946, pp. 144–145. Léal 1996, vol. I, carnet 27, sheets 2–5, 8, 62, 68–73. Léal 1996, vol. II, carnet 30, sheets 3–11, 15–39. Stein 1938, pp. 35–41. Zervos V, 212–213, 300; XXII, 339.

p. 92. *The Studio.* Paris, 1928

Laporte 1975, p. 69; cited in Burgard 1991, p. 489, n. 57. Léal 1996, vol. II, carnet 32, sheets 38–44; carnet 34, sheets 4–18, 24, 25. P.P. 27.075. Rubin 1972, pp. 128, 223–24. Rubin 1980, pp. 262–63. Zervos VII, 2, 16, 30, 37, 59, 78–79, 142.

p. 94. *Project for a Monument to Guillaume Apollinaire.* 1928

Bowness 1973, p. 139. Cooper 1967, p. 58, pls. 340, 342. Kahnweiler 1949A, n.p. Léal 1996, vol. I, carnet 27, sheets 1–10. Léal 1996, vol. II, pp. 75–77; carnet 34, sheet 23; carnet 36, sheets 8–13; carnet 37, sheets 8–27. FitzGerald 1987, *passim*. Read 1995, *passim*. Lichtenstern 1988, *passim*. Penrose 1958, pp. 49, 206, 237. Penrose 1967, pp. 21–22. Rubin 1972, p. 128. Spies 68B. Spies 1981, carnet 1044, sheets 14–20. Tucker 1970, p. 205. Withers 1978, pp. 12, 21–26. Zervos V, 342–56; VII, 94, 112, 206, 424.

p. 96. *Bather and Cabin.* Dinard, August 1928

Barr 1946, p. 150. Gasman 1981, pp. 7–39, 50, 64–66, 99, 202–04, 243–56, 254, 265, 266, 275–78, 288–98, 315–33. Léal 1996, vol. II, pp. 75–76; cat. 34, sheets 4–46. Penrose 1958, pp. 233–34. P.P. 28.171. Rubin 1972, pp. 132, 224.

Spies 67, 67A. Zervos VII, 59, 78, 79, 84–109, 187–216, 232–35.

p. 98. *Face of Marie-Thérèse.* 1928

Barr 1946, p. 158. Geiser/Baer I, 243. Mourlot 23. Rosenblum 1996, pp. 338–40, 347. Spies 130.

p. 100. *Girl Before a Mirror.* Boisgeloup, March 1932

Barr 1946, pp. 168, 176. Berger 1965, pp. 102–11, 154–62. FitzGerald 1995, pp. 202, 213–14. Penrose 1958, pp. 242–44. P.P. 32.033. Rosenblum 1996, pp. 348–59. Rubin 1972, pp. 137–40, 226–27. Zervos VII, 379.

p. 102. *Model and Sculptor with His Sculpture.* March 17, 1933

Berger 1965, pp. 158–60. Bolliger 1956, *passim*. Bowness 1973, p. 140. Geiser/Baer II, 300. Penrose 1958, pp. 244, 247. Penrose 1967, pp. 11–16.

p. 104. *Bacchanal with Minotaur.* Paris, May 18, 1933

Blind Minotaur Guided Through a Starry Night by Marie-Thérèse with a Pigeon. December 3, 1934–January 1, 1935

Faun Unveiling a Sleeping Girl. June 12, 1936

From the *Vollard Suite.* Paris, 1939

Baer 1984, *passim*. Bolliger 1956, *passim*. Chipp 1973, pp. 103–11. Galassi 1984, pp. 74, 76, 78. Geiser/Baer II, 351, 437; III, 609. Gilmour 1987, p. 84. Gilot/Lake 1964, pp. 24, 50. Léal 1996, vol. II, cat. 35, sheets 35–36. Penrose 1958, pp. 248–49. Ries 1972, *passim*. Rubin 1972, pp. 150, 230. Spies 1981, nos. 170–72, 187, 188. Zervos VIII, 100–13, 139, 285–88; IX, 96, 97.

p. 108. *Minotauromachy.* Paris, March 23, 1935

Baer 1984, p. 77. Barr 1946, pp. 192–93. Chipp 1973, pp. 103–11. Cooper 1967, p. 38; figs. 185–87, 229, 306, 309. Daix 1993A, p. 234. Geiser/Baer III, 573. Gilot/Lake 1964, pp. 24, 50. Léal 1996, vol. 2, carnet 35, sheets 41–51; carnet 38, sheets 48–50. Melville 1942, *passim*. Penrose 1958, pp. 269–70. Ries 1972, *passim*. Spies 1981, nos. 170–71, 187–88. Zervos V, 143–49, 333–38, 439–41.

p. 110. *Dream and Lie of Franco.* Paris, 1937

Barr 1946, pp. 195–97. Geiser/Baer III, 615, 616. Johnson 1980, p. 104. Penrose 1958, pp. 260, 261, 266–68. Rubin 1996, pp. 72–77. Zervos VIII, 283.

p. 112. *Maya in a Sailor Suit.* January 1938

Barr 1946, pp. 216–17, 247, 265–66, 268. Burgard 1991, p. 486. Gasman 1981, pp. 257–58. Rosenblum 1996, pp. 374–77. Seckler 1947, p. 5. Zervos IX, 104.

p. 114. *Night Fishing at Antibes.* Antibes, August 1939

Barr 1946, p. 223. Penrose 1958, pp. 288–290. Rosenthal 1983, *passim*. Rubin 1972, pp. 156, 157, 232, 233. Sabartés 1948, pp. 177–81. Spies

1981, no. 201. Zervos VIII, 323; IX, 58–61, 186–90, 194, 195, 203–06, 316.

p. 116. *Woman Dressing Her Hair.* Royan, June 1940

Berger 1965, p. 150. Brassaï 1966, pp. 42, 226. Daix 1993A, pp. 236–45, 262. Fluegel 1980, pp. 350–51. Gilot/Lake 1964, pp. 85–86, 122. Léal 1996, vol. II, pp. 142–44; carnet 43, sheets 28–40; carnet 45, sheets 7–19. Malraux 1976, p. 138. Penrose 1958, p. 296. Rubin 1972, pp. 158, 234–35. Zervos X, 302.

p. 118. *The Charnel House.* Paris, 1945

Daix 1993B, *passim*. Greenberg 1966, *passim*. Lord 1993, pp. 38–39, 325. Rubin 1972, pp. 166–69, 236–41. Rubin 1980, pp. 388–89. Zervos XIV, 76.

p. 120. *The Bull.* Paris, December 12, 1945–January 17, 1946

Gilmour 1987, pp. 85–86. Jaffé 1983, pp. 32–35. Lavin 1993, *passim*. Mourlot 17, and p. [4].

p. 124. *Woman in an Armchair.* Paris, December 30, 1948—January 16, 1949

Gilmour 1987, p. 87. Gilot/Lake 1964, pp. 37, 62–63, 216, 217, and *passim*. Mourlot 134.

p. 126. *Pregnant Woman.* Vallauris, 1950

Fluegel 1980, pp. 382–83. Gilot/Lake 1964, p. 320. Rosenblum 1983, p. 63. Rubin 1980, pp. 172, 243. Spies 349.

p. 128. *She-Goat.* Vallauris, 1950

Dufour 1969, pp. 40–41, 48–49. Gilot/Lake 1964, pp. 317–18. Penrose 1958, p. 341. Rubin 1972, pp. 174–75, 243. Spies 409.

p. 130. *Baboon and Young.* Vallauris, 1951

Berger 1965, pp. 186–201. D.B. XII, 7; d.XXI, 1, 3. Dufour 1969, p. 42. Gilot/Lake 1964, p. 319. Olivier 1965, pp. 144–45. Penrose 1958, pp. 280, 341. Rubin 1972, pp. 175, 244. Spies 463. Zervos XXII, 162.

p. 132. *Paloma and Her Doll on Black Background.* December 14, 1952

Léal 1996, vol. II, no. 30, sheets 15–39. Mourlot 229. Penrose 1958, pp. 285–86, 330. Rubin 1972, p. 410.

p. 134. *Woman by a Window.* Cannes, June 1956

Gilot/Lake 1964, p. 358. Rubin 1972, pp. 179–80, 245. Zervos XVII, 120.

p. 136. *Bull.* Cannes, c. 1958

Spies 503–08, 509, 542–45A.

p. 138.. *Plate 1* from the series *347 Gravures.* Mougins, March 1968

Barr-Sharrar 1972, *passim*. Cooper 1967, p. 78; nos. 387–88, 404–05. Dufour 1969, p. 118. Geiser/Baer VI, 1496. Schiff 1972, *passim*.

p. 140. *At Work.* 1971

Malraux 1976, pp. 4, 86. Schiff 1972, pp. 30–37. Zervos XXXIII, 145.

INDEX OF ILLUSTRATED WORKS

*This index is divided into two parts. The first
consists of works by Picasso, listed alphabetically by
title. The second section includes works by other
artists, listed alphabetically by artist. Page numbers
in bold-face type indicate works reproduced in color.*

Acknowledgments

In addition to the people mentioned on pages 6–9, numerous staff members at The Museum of Modern Art and the Los Angeles County Museum of Art have played crucial roles in the organization of this exhibition and catalogue.

At The Museum of Modern Art, we are grateful to Wendy Weitman, Associate Curator, and Deborah Dewees, former Cataloguer, in the Department of Prints and Illustrated Books; and to Kathleen Curry, Curatorial Assistant, Department of Drawings, for their assistance with the selection and presentation of works on paper. Diane Farynyk, Registrar, Ramona Bronkar Bannayan, former Associate Registrar, and Jana Joyce, Assistant Registrar, oversaw the logistics of transporting the exhibition; Cora Rosevear, Associate Curator, Department of Painting and Sculpture, and Linda Thomas, Coordinator of Exhibitions, also played key roles in the planning process. Jerome Neuner, Director of Exhibition Design and Production, Steven Jo, Production Manager and Frame Shop Coordinator, and Pedro Perez, Conservation Framer, assisted with installation and planning and reframing. James Coddington, Chief Conservator, Anny Aviram, Conservator, Karl Buchberg, Conservator, Patricia Houlihan, Associate Conservator, and Michael Duffy, Associate Conservator, assessed the physical condition and provided helpful insights into many of the works in the exhibition. Elizabeth Addison, Deputy Director for Marketing and Communications, Alexandra Partow, Assistant Director, Communications, and Uri Perrin, former Press Assistant, worked ably with their counterparts in Atlanta, Ottawa, and Los Angeles. Barbara Ross, Associate Editor in the Department of Publications, edited the manuscript for the catalogue and coordinated the complex publication process. The catalogue was designed by Antony Drobinski; Amanda Freymann and Marc Sapir, former and present production managers, oversaw its long journey from layout to print. At every stage in the organization of the exhibition and catalogue, the curators relied on the good-spirited assistance of the staff of the Department of Painting and Sculpture, especially Victoria Garvin, former Departmental Administrator, Alice Buchanan and Madeline Hensler, former and present executive secretaries, and Robert Beier, Administrative Assistant.

At the Los Angeles County Museum of Art, we are grateful for the efforts of Tom Jacobson, Acting Director of Development; Stephanie Dyas, Acting Director of Grants and Foundations; Beverley Sabo, Exhibition Programs Coordinator; Bernard Kester for his excellent exhibition design; Mitch Tuchman, Editor in Chief; Keith McKweon, Head of Media and Public Affairs, and his capable staff; Jane Burrell, Chief of Education; Bridget Cooks, Assistant Museum Educator, Special Exhibitions; Scott Taylor, graphic designer; Joseph Fronek, Senior Conservator of Paintings; Victoria Blyth-Hill, Senior Conservator of Paper; Department of Sculpture Conservation; Art Owens, Assistant Vice President, Operations; William Stahl, Head of Exhibition Construction; Jill Martinez, Curatorial Assistant, Department of Modern and Contemporary art; and the departments of the Registrar and of Technical Services.

Photograph Credits

The Baltimore Museum of Art, 20. Jan Krugier Gallery, New York, 22 left. Musée National d'Art Moderne, Centre National d'Art et de Culture Georges Pompidou, Paris, 14, 19. © Musée Picasso, Paris/© R.M.N., Agence Photographique, frontispiece, 11, 23 left, 26. Museu Picasso, Madrid, 17. Museum of Fine Arts, Houston, 23 right. The Museum of Modern Art, New York: 21, 41, 51, 57, 113, 115, 129, 135, 137, 141; photographs by David Allison, 83, 91; photograph by Tom Griesel, 111; photographs by Kate Keller, 12, 33, 35, 37, 43, 45, 47, 59, 63, 65, 67, 69, 71, 73, 75, 79, 81, 85, 87, 89, 93, 95, 97, 103, 106, 107, 109, 117, 119, 121, 122, 123, 125, 133, 139; photographs by Mali Olatunji, 49, 53, 61, 101, 131; photograph by Jim Strong, 27; photographs by Soichi Sunami, 24, 25, 39, 99, 105; photographs by Malcolm Varon, 77, 127. The Penrose Collection, 10. © Edward Quinn, 28. The Trustees of the Tate Gallery, London, 22 right.

150

Trustees of The Museum of Modern Art

151